RAMESH S.

# Let
# Life
# Flow

YogiImpressions®

**YogiImpressions®**
LET LIFE FLOW
First published in India in 2005 by
**Yogi Impressions LLP**
1711, Centre 1, World Trade Centre,
Cuffe Parade, Mumbai 400 005, India.
Website: www.yogiimpressions.com


First Edition, June 2005
Sixth reprint, September 2020

ISBN 978-93-82742-16-6


Printed at: Replika Press Pvt. Ltd.

# Contents

*Why is one unhappy? One is unhappy because almost everything one thinks – and almost everything one does – is for oneself. And truly there is no one – or another.*

# Foreword

Rishikesh, lying at the foothills of the Himalayas, is the gate through which one ascends to some of the most ancient Hindu pilgrim towns and treks on towards Gomukh – which is the source of the Ganga river. From here, the Ganga hurtles down the lofty mountains till it reaches the plains – flowing gently into Rishikesh, the first of its resting places.

It was here that I gazed on the Ganga for the first time in the spring of 2005. As I stood entranced by the sight of the last rays of the sun playing upon the flowing river, groups of young brahmachari boys, wearing saffron dhotis and kurtas, came out of the Parmarth Niketan ashram to assemble on the ghat whose marbled steps led down to the river bank. These young boys, many of whom are orphans taken into the loving fold of the ashram, began the Ganga puja by chanting mantras along with their Guru, who poured offerings into the sacred fire lit to evoke the goddess Ganga.

After this ritual they were joined by hundreds of devotees, who come here from all parts of the world, in the chanting of hymns. It was truly astounding to see them singing along in fluent Sanskrit and Hindi with equal devotion and felicity. This amazing confluence of cultures on the banks of the Ganga is a sight to behold, every evening.

The chanting reaches a crescendo and culminates in the lighting of huge brass lamps with innumerable wicks that burn brightly as the Ganga 'aarti' is being performed. Facing the worshippers is a serene, larger-than-life statue of Lord Shiva absorbed in meditation while the gurgling Ganga flows merrily behind. This is Shiva as Pure Consciousness – silently witnessing Itself being worshipped by Its own creation.

What strikes one at first is that this is an aarti being performed for a living God, as embodied in a river. It is an awe-inspiring sight... this daily ritual and devout worship of what many, in other parts of the world, might consider as 'just a river'. Heraclitus said, "You could not step twice into the same river," and one only needs to realise that it truly is a different Ganga that is being worshipped every evening – alive, vibrant, continuously renewing. It is indeed this unceasing change, which is the very basis of life and living, that is being worshipped. And this is what *Let Life Flow* is all about.

Ramesh Balsekar says that life is like a deep river, flowing incessantly, whereas the day-to-day living for most people is a preference for the security and stagnancy of the little pools beside the river. The river presents an apt metaphor for his concept that no one is a doer but, rather, all actions are happenings ordained by the One Source, who some refer to as God. To perceive ourselves as the doers is like the river thinking that it is pushing itself onwards to the sea, or the sea thinking that the tides are its own doing – totally oblivious of the fact that it is the gravitational force of the moon that is responsible for their ebb and flow.

Leonardo Da Vinci said, "When you put your hand in a flowing stream, you touch the last that has gone before and the first of what is still to come." *Let Life Flow* shows you how to be the still hand in the flowing stream.

Gautam Sachdeva
April 2005

# Introduction

The stress and strain of day-to-day living, especially modern living in urban areas, has to be considered and dealt with at two levels. One is at the surface of living from moment to moment, and the other, perhaps even much more important and at a much deeper level, is being anchored in peace and harmony while facing life from moment to moment.

Many years ago, I was taken to a place in Los Angeles which specifically dealt with the first variety of stress. The place offered a number of devices and gadgets specially designed to substantially reduce the stress of daily living on executives functioning at a higher level in various aspects of life, such as finance, business, and politics. The membership was expensive and, therefore, exclusive.

The executive club was equipped with diverse items ranging from a massage table and a saltwater tank that could keep people afloat without any effort at all, to physical and mental games for the specific purpose of reducing physical and mental stress and strain. Good music would fall in this category as a great reliever of mental stress. The idea was for the members to visit on weekends, if they could not do so on working days, to reduce the stress accumulated during the week – and, one supposes, to be ready to take on the stress of the following week.

At this superficial or surface level of life, various activities could be of help: yoga, meditation, light massage, belly laughter, and various other physical and psychological treatments. But these cannot reach the deepest level to enable you to feel anchored in peace and harmony, a state in which you never feel uncomfortable with yourself or with others, while you face life from moment to moment. This is a state in which anger may arise in the moment, but would never make you feel enmity or hatred towards the person (body-mind organism) that was the cause of the anger arising as an immediate natural or biological reaction.

The only way you could have this lasting feeling of hating neither yourself nor anyone else – always being comfortable with yourself and with others – is when you are totally convinced, beyond the shadow of a doubt, that no one, neither you yourself nor anyone else, could ever be the doer of any action; that all action can never be anything done by anyone, but a happening that simply could not have not happened according to the universal cosmic law.

This understanding means, in effect, being anchored in peace and harmony while facing life from moment to moment. Facing life from moment to moment means accepting life as it happens, whatever the moment brings – pain or pleasure – without getting involved in it by resisting it. What it means, in effect, is to witness whatever happens, doing whatever needs to be done (knowing that that it is a happening according to the cosmic law) and, most importantly, being still. Being still means not thinking, not conceptualising in the past or future – being still in the present moment.

The state of being anchored in peace and tranquillity, while facing life from moment to moment, is indeed the result of the realisation that all action is a divine happening and not anyone's action. Such a realisation of non-doership immediately means the total absence of shame and guilt for one's own supposed actions, and also the total absence of any hatred and malice, jealousy and envy, towards any 'other'. This state of being anchored in tranquillity and repose, by its very nature, includes the acceptance of whatever happens from moment to moment in daily living, and thus, the question of stress and strain in daily living simply cannot arise.

It is a fact of life that the sting of life's slings and arrows is astonishingly short; so also, the mellow glow from a week or two of holidays will fade just as surely. Happiness, many psychologists are concluding, seems to be largely determined by the genes and not by outside reality. However tragic or comic life's ups and downs, people appear to return inexorably to whatever happiness level is pre-set in their constitution.

The idea is similar to the set-point concept in weight-control, a theory that says the brain seems to be wired to turn the body's metabolism up or down to maintain a pre-set weight. There is also, scientists contend, a set point for happiness – a genetically determined mood level that the vagaries of life may nudge upward or downward, but only for a while. With time, the grouchy tend to become as cranky as before and the light-hearted, cheery again.

Interviews with a range of psychologists show that the idea of a biological set-point for a sense of well-being (quite apart form being anchored in peace and harmony while facing life from moment to moment) has wide support in the field. Says Dr. Jerome Kagan, a developmental psychologist at Harvard University: "It's clear that T. S. Eliot was by nature dour and Jay Leno is congenitally upbeat. But we are far from filling in the biological blanks."

The set-point idea seems to make sense of long-standing data on happiness that has puzzled researchers. Studies of happiness in several countries have found that money makes little difference in perceptions of happiness, except among the very poor. Nor does education, or marriage and a family, or any of the other variables that researchers have sought to correlate with contentment.

Each factor may make a person a little happier, but it has a minor impact, compared with the individual's characteristic sense of well-being.

Says Dr. Edward Diener, a psychologist at the University of Illinois: "We find that for events like being promoted or losing a lover, most of the effect on people's mood is gone by three months, and there's not a trace by six months." He cites data showing that lottery winners are no happier a year after their good fortune than they were before. And several studies show that even people with spinal-cord injuries tend to rebound in spirits.

All this, of course, can relate only to the superficial level of daily living. To be anchored in a deep sense of peace and harmony, while facing the various vicissitudes of life from day to day, is an altogether different matter. Such anchorage depends almost entirely on the conditioning of the individual concerned, a conditioning that reflects the total acceptance of the fact that the free will of the individual human being is, in fact, illusory. All human action is entirely a happening that simply could not have not happened, strictly according to a cosmic law, according to which everything in the universe moves – from a small object to the stars and planets in the sky.

It is a proven fact that the thought and the relevant action cannot really be separated. The thought and the act are one integral whole, and the human being has no control over the arising of the thought.

# ONE

# The Essence
## of
## Life and Living

'Let life flow': what does it really mean? More pertinently, what does it *not* mean? It does *not* mean being lazy and not doing what one is supposed to be doing; it does *not* mean 'slacking off'. It also does *not* mean being insensitive to other people's misfortunes, with the attitude, "so what? that's life." What it does mean, in general terms, is to go about one's daily routine with a relaxed attitude, based on the total basic understanding that nothing at all can happen unless it is supposed to happen according to one's destiny, according to the Will of God, according to the cosmic law. In other words, one goes through one's daily routine, whatever it is in our given situation, making our decisions as responsibly as it is in our nature to do, putting in our best efforts to put our decisions into action in the given circumstances. Having done whatever it is that one can do, what this basic understanding does is to relieve us of the unconscionable load of worry and anxiety about what might happen in the future.

Even more important, perhaps, is the fact that the basic understanding that no one is a doer – that, in the words of the Buddha, "events happen, deeds are done, consequences happen, but there is no individual doer of any deed" – in one moment, relieves us of the usual load of guilt and shame for our 'immoral' or unsuccessful actions, and pride and arrogance for our success. Also, perhaps more importantly, we know that we simply do not have to carry the usual burden of hatred and malice towards the 'other' whom we would otherwise consider to be the cause of our hurt or misfortune. The understanding is based on the total acceptance that if we are hurt, we are hurt because, for some reason which we simply cannot know, we were supposed to be hurt according to the all-pervading cosmic law that applies to everything in the universe, from the smallest atom to the largest planet or star. In other words, it would be downright stupid to hate anyone – any particular body-mind organism – through which the act that hurt us had happened, again, according to the same cosmic law.

'Let life flow' simply means a) accepting whatever is in the moment as something that could never have not happened, b) doing whatever we think we need to do in the moment, and c) without loading our mind unnecessarily with a load of conceptualising about what might or might not happen in the uncertain future.

A simple potter named Gora, in the 13th century in Maharashtra (India), much loved as a poet-saint, wrote a poem which states very simply what is meant by 'letting life flow'. Gora says:

"May Thy form always be in my heart,
    and Thy name on my lips.
The body is subject to the natural laws of
    phenomenality.
Let it do the work assigned to it by Nature.
Body-mind organisms can only react
    according to the way they are programmed.
I truly accept that for the individual
    there is no other ordained rule of good conduct.
All actions happen strictly according to Thy Will.
Having truly understood this, I have surrendered
    at your feet all my being and actions.
May the 'I Am' in this body soar into the sky,
    and not get involved in phenomenal functioning.
Gora recites your name with deep feeling,
    without any expectation of any sort."

Indeed, a little reflection would show us that the basis of free living is a strong, innate, unsentimental compassion for human beings unnecessarily suffering and perishing from their very efforts to save themselves. Living happens, no one to be saved.

Gora's simple, practical philosophy of life and living brings clearly into prominence the wrong impression among many Westerners that the 'Oriental mind' is mysterious, irrational, and inscrutable. What Gora says is strictly from personal experience, but the general tendency of the educated seeker is to want proof for the concept. This attitude ignores the basic fact that 'knowledge of reality' cannot be had by cumbersome calculations of theology, metaphysics and logical inference. For Gora, life can only be understood directly and not in terms of representational thinking, which, in any case, the simple potter was not capable of!

What Gora suggests is a certain spontaneity in action and not a protest against convention. To be free from conventional knowledge and standards is not to spurn it but to be not deceived by it.

'Letting life flow' is a view that liberates the human mind from its constricting identification with the abstract ego as the doer. The doing happens, and there should really be no difficulty in knowing this because we would admit that we 'know' how to move our hands, how to make a decision, or how to breathe, even though we can hardly begin to explain in words how we do it. *We know how to do it because we just do it: because it happens.* To realise that living just happens is an extension of this kind of knowledge, which gives us a very different view of ourselves from that to which we are conventionally accustomed.

We think we make our own decisions, based on our conventional culture, knowledge, and experience. We feel that we decide rationally because we base our decisions on the available relevant data on the subject.

But we might well ask ourselves if we really know what information is relevant as our plans are constantly upset by unforeseen events. Then again, we would never know if the available information is enough or what research is in the pipeline. And, finally, after having gone through the motions of gathering information in a rational way, on the spur of the moment, just because of a 'hunch' – or because we are just plainly tired of thinking – we act.

The fact of the matter is that the rigorously scientific method of predicting the future can be applied only in special cases, where prompt action is not urgent. By far the greater part of our important decisions depends upon a 'hunch' – upon the 'peripheral vision' of the mind. Thus, the reliability of our decisions rests upon our natural talent to 'feel' the situation, upon the degree to which this 'peripheral vision' has been developed. When we know this from our own experience of daily living, should it be so difficult to envisage that our decision could be inextricably intertwined with such decisions being made elsewhere by others in different places, all over the world, in that instant?!

Experience in making decisions by intuition might well show that this 'peripheral' aspect of mind works best when our minds do not try to interfere with it, when we trust it to work by itself spontaneously, when we 'let life flow'.

Peripheral vision works most effectively when we do not look at things directly but out of the corners of the eyes. Similarly, when we are trying to see the details of a distant object, the eyes automatically relax, not *trying* to see. So also, in order to taste our food – and enjoy it more intensely – we cannot *use* the muscles of the mouth and tongue; we must trust them to do the work themselves. The whole point is that we must relax the sharp and staring kind of sight before we can regain the powers of peripheral vision. It is not simply calmness of the mind, but, more importantly, the 'non-graspingness' of the mind that is of significance. As Chuang-Tse has put it: "The perfect man employs his mind as a mirror. It grasps nothing; it refuses nothing. It receives but does not keep."

The important point is that the centre of the mind's activity is not in the ego, not in the conscious thinking process. 'Letting life flow' is what happens when the mind is allowed to function in the integrated, spontaneous way that is natural to it. Similarly, everything is to be judged not by its conformity with purely theoretical standards but by the concrete content of the experience. In other words, 'letting life flow' happens when the astonishing ingenuity and creative power of man's spontaneous and natural functioning is not blocked by one's trying to master it in terms of formal methods and technique. It is like the skill of the centipede in using a hundred legs at the same time:

"The centipede was happy, quite
Until a toad in fun
Said, 'pray, which leg goes after which?'
This worked his mind to such a pitch,
He lay distracted in a ditch,
Considering how to run."

The whole point about 'letting life flow' – the marvellous quality of spontaneous action – is that it is perfectly human, and yet shows no sign of being contrived.

It is part of the pattern of the mind that it can, as it were, stand aside from life and reflect upon it, that it can be aware of its own existence and, amazingly, it can criticise its own processes: the mind has something resembling a 'feedback' system. The problem, however, is that the system can be frustrated by its own complexity. Thus, it might take so long for the information to pass through: when human beings think too carefully and minutely about an action to be taken, they cannot make up their minds in time to act, and the system gets paralysed. When a human being becomes so self-conscious, so self-controlled that he cannot let go of himself, he dithers and wobbles between two opposites.

In other words, when the desire for certainty and security prompts identification between the mind and its own image of itself, it gets split; it cannot let go of itself. To cling to an image of always remaining 'good' or 'happy' is to be in constant contradiction and conflict.

Hence, the action must always prevail as against constant reflection – acting spontaneously on its own, into the unknown. 'Don't wobble' is the final instruction the mind must give itself, which of course results in spontaneous action. And, naturally, it is the deep understanding that nothing can actually happen unless it is the Will of God – according to the cosmic law – that allows the spontaneous action to happen. In other words, 'letting life flow' means liberation from the dualism of thought and action. It means, in effect, not an anti-intellectual exclusion of thinking, but an action on any level whatsoever, physical or psychic, without trying, at the same moment, to observe and check from outside (the wobbling).

The same holds true of the relationship between feeling and action. Not content with feeling happy, one wants to feel oneself feeling happy (am I sure I am having fun?). It is basically important to understand that no amount of care and hesitancy, no amount of responsible introspection and searching of our motives, can ever make any ultimate difference to the fact that the mind is 'like an eye that sees but cannot see itself'. In the end, the only alternative to a shuddering paralysis – a nervous breakdown – is to leap into action after all the responsible introspection has been done, regardless of the consequences, because it is actually impossible to do anything else. And, again, this would seem amazingly easy if we are able to accept totally that nothing can ultimately happen unless it is the Will of God.

## LIFE IS A SERIES OF SITUATIONS

You face a certain situation at a certain time; you are not sure how to deal with it effectively in view of the conflicting possibilities; you do not know what the 'proper' thing would be to do; you get into a panic, and finally watch yourself doing something or the other. And after that, you are apprehensive about the consequences of what has been done, and pretty soon, another situation that needs your attention has developed. This chain of events and situations becomes life itself and, before you know it, you get a heart attack. An extreme case, you say. But is it really such an extreme case, or is it the typical case, with slight variations, among the reasonably comfortable social strata, wherein one's wants are ever on the increase?

In other words, life would actually seem to be a series of situations needing one's attention almost continuously, and one would specifically have to seek and hope to find a few bits and pieces of peace and tranquillity in between these situations. But is there an alternative? Does the alternative lie between living as a responsible hardworking citizen or living one's life as an irresponsible, happy-go-lucky individual? Would it ever be possible, in the urban world of today, to feel anchored in peace and harmony while facing life's situations as they happen from moment to moment? In other words, would it ever be possible to live one's life with tranquillity and repose as the base, while dealing with life's situations as they happen on the surface from moment to moment? Is this a feasible possibility or is it just a dream, an illusion?

It is not too difficult to imagine a life situation in which a strong emotion like anger could arise in the moment and yet not be carried forward in horizontal time as animosity, fury, rage, or wrath. Similarly, worry in the moment need not necessarily be carried forward into anxiety in horizontal time; an event, a happening, could certainly produce grief in the moment, but should it necessarily prolong itself into mourning?

This kind of acceptance of the emotion in the moment, without involvement in duration, is certainly not impossible. It has happened in the past, and is happening now, though in comparatively rare instances. It would seem that what is really needed is a drastic change in the mindset. It is quite a simple thing to realise that what pushes the emotion in the moment into involvement in duration is the fact that the ego reacts to the natural reaction in the body-mind organism. In other words, the natural, biological reaction in the body-mind organism to something seen or heard, or to a thought arising in the mind, is essentially not in anyone's control: it depends entirely on the particular programming in the body-mind organism (genes plus conditioning). This impersonal reaction in the moment is turned into personal involvement in duration when the ego reacts to the natural reaction in the body-mind organism and identifies the reaction as its own reaction: the anger arising naturally, spontaneously, in the body-mind organism is converted into: *I am angry; so and so made me angry; I hate him....*

Therefore, it is clear that there is no involvement if the ego is able to keep away from the natural emotion, and is thus able merely to witness the arising and falling away of the emotion as something which has arisen in a body-mind organism, not 'in me'. The involvement means one hates oneself for what has happened and also, at the same time, one hates the 'other' as the cause of what happened. Life, as a series of situations, then means a continuous addition to the load of hatred of oneself and for the 'other'. And this is truly the suffering in life that one wants to get rid of. It is not something called pain – physical, psychological, or financial – that might appear and disappear from moment to moment. The absence of the load of hatred means truly being anchored in peace and harmony, while facing life from moment to moment: never being uncomfortable with oneself, never being uncomfortable with others at any moment.

Being anchored in peace and harmony while facing life from moment to moment means: Being still while the Primal Energy functions through the body, bringing about physical and mental movements that are merely witnessed as something happening, and not as something being 'done' by oneself or the 'other'. And this is what is meant by the words: 'let life flow'.

# Human Conflict
# and
# Unhappiness

When and why does the spiritual seeking begin?

A child lives in his own little world of magic, perfectly content to live with his parents and his toys. He is not concerned either with time or the outside world. He is not concerned with achieving something or being someone special in the outside world.

A friend of mine told me about his three-year-old daughter who saw a little mouse slip into their apartment and then quickly slip out. She was intrigued; she wanted to know where the mouse lived; and when she was told that he lived in a hole at the bottom of the house, she promptly asked whether the little mouse also had toys of his own!

The child grows up into a world of separation: separate name, separate parents, a choice of toys, a choice of food.... In other words, the child discovered a world in which time and space, and separation, made certain demands on her: making a choice between alternatives available, some needs and desires not being satisfied, which she could not understand. She began to know the outside world, which demanded explanation, exploration, effort, a certain amount of manipulation in her pursuit of pleasure and avoidance of pain and frustration: an entirely different world, which made it necessary to ask questions and get information that would be required for her to adjust herself to this new environment. It was exciting.

The child also begins to find herself in areas never known before. What is this thing called 'being dead'? I remember my granddaughter asking her father: "What is dying?" – she had heard about some friend of her father being dead the previous day. The child would probably have been satisfied with a fairly simple explanation, but the father chose to treat her as a grown-up and gave her a little dissertation on birth and death. The intelligent child listened attentively and, finally, announced: "I am never going to die" – a deeply intuitive, unrecognised oneness with the creation as a whole.

As the child grows up, the conditioning increases. She is told – and comes to believe – that if she is honest and hardworking, she will always succeed in life and be happy. Her actual experience, however, shows her that honesty and hard work do not always lead to success, and that the creed, "As you sow, so you reap" also does not always work. Her experience is that someone sows and, very often, someone else reaps! This gap between expectation and result creates a lot of confusion and frustration. In her teens, thus, a child is a lost child, without any direction.

The fact of the matter is that life is not such a simple straightforward affair, and unless one is aware of the fundamentals of 'life' as it happens, confusion and frustration simply cannot be avoided. The basic fundamental of life, as we know it, is that the essence of all manifestation is continuous change from birth towards death, in horizontal time, as distinguished from the present moment. As soon as a sentient being is 'born', whether it is an insect, bird, animal, or man – the animated consciousness infuses in the creature the will to live, not to yield to death. This is the infamous ego, the identification of the individual organism with the will not to let go of the life that it is. Later on, the infusion includes 'free will', the sense of personal doership together with the intellect for the human being.

In the absence of intellect, while the animal's ego is certainly aware of the irreconcilable opposition between 'me' and 'not-me' (or the 'other'), between pleasure and suffering, the animal cannot think or feel this duality; the animal cannot be intellectually conscious of the difference between pleasure and pain in the absence of the actual physical circumstances. But man can, and does, conceptualise about the future satisfaction of these physical and psychological needs. It is this element that creates a feeling of conflict, disharmony and unhappiness in man but not in the animal.

This is one part of the double-bind. The other part consists of the fact that while the animal has no feelings of guilt in its efforts to maintain and preserve its own life, the dubious gift of intellect in man gives him the clear perception that mere persevering to exist is not his real purpose in life. Intellect compels him to see, at least intellectually, that he must necessarily be something very much more than his psychosomatic organism, and therefore compels him to seek his 'true identity', which he intuitively knows as infinity, intemporality, immutability. The double-bind consists in the fact that man continues to think of his true nature only in terms that his intellect can understand – in terms of achievement. In other words, man imagines his true nature within the framework of animal affectivity – a state where happiness will reign supreme with limitless good food, unbounded sexual vigour, unrivalled physical and intellectual capacity, etc.: in fact, the state of being in paradise!

The significance of this 'desire' of man to 'attain' the perfect affective life needs to be clearly analysed and understood in order to go to the root of the problem of seeking-seeker-sought, the problem of human conflict and unhappiness. The fundamental fault in such thinking – the desire for perfection in the framework of living – is in forgetting that the entire phenomenality is an appearance in consciousness, an appearance based on polaric duality, in which happiness and unhappiness are inseparably interdependent.

Indeed, the bondage consists entirely in the 'desire' to 'attain' something. The liberation, therefore, can consist in simply apperceiving that any desire – whether for some material benefit or even for spiritual enlightenment – is itself the real and only obstruction. In other words, man wants harmony but he wants it in terms of living this life; he understands that there must be a 'Being' at the end of this 'living', but he can only think of that 'Being' in terms of this 'living' without its sorrows. He simply cannot apperceive the fact that to arrive at the 'Being' – which he already is, the seeker is already the sought – all that has to happen is that 'living' as he knows it, has to be given up. And this can happen only when man accepts totally, without the slightest doubt, that nothing can be 'achieved' by personal effort but that it has to happen according to a cosmic law, which no man can ever possibly comprehend.

Man wants to continue his 'living' and his 'doing', and at the same time he demands his 'Being'. Man will not give up war, but needs, and wants, and demands peace! Man is not prepared to let go – and that is the only problem. Man wants to wake up to reality, his 'true nature', but will not give up the dreamed reality. Man forgets that the ultimate goal of life, if as such it can be called, is not 'becoming' something, but 'non-becoming', non-doing, non-living – a letting go of his phenomenality through merely witnessing life happening through every body-mind instrument: Being still, 'letting life flow'.

In order to understand the problem of human conflict and unhappiness, it is absolutely necessary to have a clear apprehension of the basic difference between the concept of duality and the concept of dualism. Duality is the very basis of the manifestation; the principle of polaric duality, the existence of interrelated opposites of every nature. In duality, the opposites – life and death, light and darkness, good and evil – are not at war with each other. Dualism means pursuing happiness to the exclusion of all unhappiness; pursuing triumph to the exclusion of all defeat, pursuing what is good to the banishment of all that is considered evil – in short, the pursuit of health, wealth, and happiness to the absolute exclusion of sickness, poverty, and pain. This can only mean frustration and disharmony more often than not. The principle of polaric duality, on the other hand, means the willing acceptance of the interrelated opposites as the very basis of both the universe and life therein.

In the acceptance of polaric duality as the very basis of life, life becomes an art, holding the two interrelated opposites in harmonious balance. As Lao-Tzu put it, "Knowing the male and keeping the female, one becomes a universal stream; becoming a universal stream, one is not separated from eternal virtue." Male and female, of course, refer not so much to sex as to the dominant

17

characteristics in the masculine and the feminine. The interrelated opposites, in other words, are like the opposite but inseparable sides of a coin, the poles of a magnet, or the pulse and the interval in any vibration.

While the exercise of volition and personal effort in the separation of dualism results in turning life into one mad hectic rush, a real understanding of the polaric nature of duality gives life a cyclical serenity, as illustrated by the ancient Taoist story of a farmer whose horse ran away:

> *When the neighbours gathered that evening to console him about his bad luck, the farmer said 'maybe'; the next day the horse returned to the farm and brought with him half a dozen wild horses, and when the neighbours again got together to congratulate him on his good fortune, the farmer again said 'maybe'; the third day, his son broke a leg when he tried to saddle and ride one of the wild horses. To the expressions of sympathy from neighbours, the farmer said 'maybe'. The following day, the conscription officers came to the village to recruit young men for the army, but the farmer's son was rejected because of his broken leg. Again the neighbours arrived in the evening and said how good it was that everything had ended so well. The farmer said 'maybe'.*

According to the principle of the polaric duality of opposites, not only does life mean a continuous cycle of good and bad events which prevents monotony and makes living a wondrous affair, but nature has very conveniently provided our psychosomatic systems with alternating states of sleeping and waking, forgetting and remembering.

When the *Book of Genesis* refers to the fall from grace of Adam and Eve because they gained the 'knowledge of good and evil', the meaning is that their fall was due to a discrimination between 'good and bad', 'useful and useless', 'acceptable and unacceptable', due to a concern about what is of advantage and what is not in the prevailing environment. In other words, man brings in unhappiness for himself when he shows an obsessive preoccupation with security and survival. On the other hand, acceptance of the polaric duality on which life and nature is based would mean a oneness with the universe that enables one to live one's life with a serenity that would increase the chances of security and survival for the very reason that there is no anxiety that could hamper and curb the free movement in whatever one is doing.

What this really means, in effect, is that man's conflict and unhappiness are based on two interrelated misconceptions: one, that he is separate and distinct from the rest of the manifestation, and two, that in the functioning of the manifestation, he has independence and choice of action in determining the results and events. There is truly no entity as an individual either to exercise free will or to suffer destiny: the functioning – seeing, hearing, etc. happen through the psychosomatic mechanism; there is truly no 'we' to live our lives, but 'living' happens through the various psychosomatic mechanisms or body-mind organisms.

It is rather a curious fact that man craves for certainty and security for himself as an intrinsic part of happiness, but has no clear idea of what this 'himself' is. This 'himself' (or 'myself') is in effect merely an identification between the mind and the self-image, an image that is really only an abstract of memories of events over the past. Indeed, it is this censored and edited abstract that is considered as the individual; it is more concerned with the past rather than the present, and the future happiness that he desires is very much related to the certainty and security based on the past. Thus, for instance, someone makes financial and social investments based on past experience, together with a careful assessment of the future prospects based on conventional standards; and it is not uncommon that in spite of all calculations, his investments turn out to be a ghastly failure, whereas someone else who has certainly not ignored his past experience but has not disregarded his 'hunch', has done remarkably well.

It is almost everyone's experience that man attaches undue importance to past conventions, conscious thinking, communication by linear signs and mathematical symbols, and not nearly enough to the intelligent, intuitive 'feel' – far more to the central spotlight vision and not to the peripheral vision, far more to the analytical data and not enough to the 'gut-feeling'. It is really not a matter of one or the other but a matter of one complementing the other. What happens most of the time is that the conditioning of conventionality is so powerful that it smothers spontaneity: this, unfortunately, can be seen in the education of a child, where the stress on abstract, linear thinking combined with social conventions sometimes reaches such a degree of repression of the child's inherent spontaneity of expression that it does positive harm to the child. What is necessary is certainly not a surrender to a mad urge of caprice, but a rational recognition of an intelligence that does not base itself on too orderly a working of reason and intellect, an intelligence than can be clearly seen in the way our body functions, the way we are able to move our limbs, and take our breath. Man is afraid to rely on the spontaneous functioning with which he is naturally endowed but which gets blocked when restrained in its natural working by any effort to understand it in terms of conventional techniques.

## ARISING OF THOUGHTS

Thoughts, and even desires, arise in the mind not only of the ordinary person but also in the mind of the sage because it is the nature of the mind to receive whatever is offered; but there the similarity ends. While the ordinary person gets involved in them either by trying to grasp and hold them or reject them, the sage does not pursue them, he leaves them alone. The point, of course, is that any attempt to stop thoughts from arising, apart from the futility of effort and the resulting frustration, divides the mind into that which tries to stop and the mind that resists, and thus there is conflict. Thoughts arise because of the continuous conditioning that takes place and the mnemonic impressions that are thereby created – to try to erase them consciously and deliberately is like 'washing blood with blood'. The point is simple: thoughts arise but, being without substance, they promptly vanish if they are not accepted and pursued as effective reality. Any positive effort to control the mind or let go of oneself only strengthens the ego; spontaneity and purposeful intention are contradictory terms.

The situation is precisely what is indicated by the classic instance of the effectiveness of the medicine depending on not thinking of a monkey while ingesting the medicine: the condition itself becomes the mnemonic impression of the monkey which promptly arises whenever the medicine is about to be taken. This is the kind of double-bind in which man finds himself almost every moment if he thinks and acts as an individual entity. The only answer is to be able to accept absolutely that, in the words of the Buddha, "events happen, deeds are done, but there is no individual doer thereof."

The only answer to the question "at any moment, what am I supposed to do?" would be: do whatever you think you should do, with the total understanding that there cannot be any individual doer. Whatever action results thereafter will be the spontaneous, natural (divine) action because then no individual entity would be concerned in it. An indication of such apperception would be a distinct feeling, not of frustration arising from the sense of volition but of utter freedom. As a Zen Master put it: "Nothing is left to you then but to have a good laugh." It has been known that such a feeling of total relief and joy has so destroyed the separation between the Master and the disciple that they have sometimes ended up by rolling on the ground in uncontrollable laughter, unreasonable mirth, and joy.

What happens at such a time is that the prison walls of *dualism* suddenly collapse and one finds oneself in an altogether different world, with the sudden realisation that it is indeed spontaneous, non-volitional action that has been happening all along and that personal volition was only an illusion. It is as if one has been in the stream of life, being carried along, and the apparent effort of trying to swim against the current was not only totally ineffective but wholly unnecessary. In other words, dualism between the self and the 'other', between the observer and the observed, between the seeker and the sought, disappears in the apperception that both are objects being lived – in the dream play that is 'living': all there is, is 'thinking', 'doing', 'experiencing', without any individual doer doing any of those things. Here is what the Arabian sage Monoimus has to say about self-realisation:

> "Learn whence is sorrow and joy, and love and hate, and waking though one would not, and sleeping though one would not, and falling in love though one would not.
>
> And if thou shouldst closely investigate all these things, thou wilt find God in Thyself, one and many,

just as the atom:
Thus finding in Thyself a way out of Thyself."

All dualism is illusion, all action is spontaneous, and all volition is an illusion. Once this is clearly realised, one ceases to find the perfect solution. Seeing the illusoriness of volition makes all action precisely what is supposed to happen according to the Will of God, according to the cosmic law. By the same token, it becomes clear that it truly needs no specific effort, through any strenuous disciplines or practices or devices – such as any repeated affirmation of any formulas or thoughts or words or actions, in order to see something that has always been there. The Tao philosophy calls all effort to realise Tao as "putting legs on a snake" because everything is Tao.

The final proof of the apperception of Truth is that all questions and doubts have disappeared; in fact, all thought and thinking about Truth have disappeared, obviously because one has *become* the Truth. This has nothing to do with talking about Truth with someone who comes for help: even here, there is the complete acceptance that no one is a speaker, no one is a listener – the speaking and listening has been happening through two apparently separate body-mind instruments. This is very similar to a man who is working hard, with concentration, at his regular daily tasks, but never has to remind himself during this period about his name and where he stays.

Similarly, in any game or sport, once the basics have been grasped, success depends almost entirely on the extent to which these basics do *not* enter the mind during the entire performance. And, of course, the extent to which this happens in any particular case would obviously depend on what might be called the 'destiny' of that body-mind organism or the Will of God, according to a cosmic law.

It must be stated, again and again, that the understanding has to be allowed to flower and blossom by itself without any interference from the intellect (this would, of course, depend upon the destiny of the body-mind organism concerned). As Nisargadatta Maharaj would point out, persistent and constant raising of problems and questions would be like scratching oneself at a particular spot, and thereby causing an itch that was not there in the first place! The fish lives in the water but he is not mindful of the water; the bird flies in the air but knows not of the wind. The fish has no questions about the nature of the water, nor the bird about the nature of the wind!

The teaching, Tao or Vedanta, in its concepts, is like a thorn that is used to remove the notion of desire for material security (or even self-realisation) that is like a thorn in the skin. But if that teaching is used to seek spiritual security for the individual, one thorn merely gets replaced by another. Pure understanding is all; apperception is the end, not the means to achieve something; to seek life, the living has to be destroyed, the 'one' doer must die.

# THREE

# Non-action is the Correct Action

Non-action means being still.

Non-action, from the viewpoint of just *beingness*, articulates into correct action on the phenomenal plane: this could be anything from inaction to violent action. The majority of our actions happen to be, however, what may be called incorrect actions insofar as doing unnecessary things, terrified of not doing any action – inaction – and obsessed with the necessity of 'doing' something. We seem to be totally unaware of the possible consequences of not doing anything: something happening!

Actually, as a matter of fact, what we regard as action is very often merely the natural, biological reaction in the body-mind organism when one of the senses comes into contact with its relevant object (e.g. when the eyes see something or the ears hear something). The ego then reacts to the natural reaction, and feels proud or guilty, and considers itself the doer. Non-action is spontaneous and, therefore, correct action.

> *Two monks were once travelling together, when they came to a stream. They were about to wade into the stream when they saw a young woman standing near the edge without the courage to cross it. One monk went straight on, ignoring the woman deliberately. The other one stopped and asked the woman if she needed any help. When she said she did, he picked her up in his arms, took her over to the other bank, and sat her down. He bid her goodbye and went to join the other monk who was waiting for him with an angry expression. He did not say anything, and the two set off on their journey. When they reached the lodging temple for their stay overnight, the angry colleague could restrain himself no longer, and said to the other, "You know we are not supposed to go near females, especially not the young and pretty ones. You know it is dangerous. Why did you do that?"*
>
> *"I left the woman at the other bank," came the answer. "Why are you still carrying her?"*

In the case of a sage, the ego, totally devoid of the sense of personal doership, does not react to the natural reaction of the body-mind organism. And hence, all his actions are correct actions, whatever the consequences according to the cosmic law. Correct actions can only be spontaneous actions, "the product of the split-second that outwits the fraud of Time."

Perhaps we would be more accurate if we said that correct action is 'adequate' action, and incorrect, unnecessary action is 'inadequate' action. As the French writer St. Exupery has put it, "Perfection is attained, not when there is nothing more to be added, but when there is nothing more to be taken away."

It seems to be a human weakness to be so obsessed with working – doing – that it is taken as a matter of course that everyone must be seen to be 'doing' something all the time. Inaction is considered to be laziness, a vice. But it is a matter of proven fact that, as one psychologist put it, "at least fifty percent of the activities in question are futile even to us, and probably about nine-tenths are ultimately considered superfluous." It is really questionable if more than a small percentage is fundamentally necessary, let alone beneficial. In actual fact, 'doing' happens to be a running away, an escape from reality.

> *The schoolmaster took a nap every afternoon but the children were not allowed to do so at any time. He explained his own habitual practice by telling the children, "I go to dreamland every afternoon to meet the old sages and get instructions from them."*
>
> *One afternoon it was so hot that some of the children simply could not stay awake, and were forced to take a nap. The schoolmaster was very angry and demanded an explanation for disobeying his instructions. Everyone kept quiet but one boy stood up and explained, "I went*

*to dreamland and met the sages and asked them if our*
*schoolmaster met them every afternoon for instruction, but*
*they all said that they had never seen any such fellow."*

To the average person, the alternative to 'doing'
is 'idleness', but, in fact, the real alternative to 'doing' is
'being'. Behind action and inaction – the base of both
– lies non-action. If we only knew how to BE, all our
actions would be necessary actions – work in its pure sense
done through the working mind; more importantly, our
passivity would then be not idleness but dynamic inaction,
very much necessary as a part of 'action', not realised as
serenity and harmony.

Non-action of the sage is in the medium of what could
appropriately be called 'being still' – silence – but this
silence is not the negative state that is usually associated
with that term. On the contrary it is highly positive, potent,
dynamic. Indeed, for those who have the receptivity
for it, it is often felt as 'radiation' – a terrific impact.

The *Bhagavad Gita* tells us quite a lot about the nature
of action.

We are told:
1) "The world is imprisoned in its own activity
   except when actions are performed as worship of
   God; therefore, you must perform every action
   sacramentally, and be free from all attachments
   to results."

2) "You have the right to work, but only for the sake of the work; you have no right to the fruits of work. Desire for the fruits of work must never be your motive in working."

3) "They who work selfishly for results are miserable."

To the modern man, this is not comprehensible! The modern man obviously works for what he can earn. In fact, he perhaps goes to the other extreme: he has no right to work unless he gets paid for the work done. Indeed, what has become sacramental is not the work but the remuneration: payment for work or service of any kind, however badly done. Actually, it is not difficult to draw a simple meaning for Lord Krishna's advice: do not work with the results in mind. If you do, you are likely to be disappointed and frustrated because, whatever your efforts, the results have never been in your control. Therefore, why not do your best, forget the results (or fruits) over which you have no control, and take on the next job or work?

*A soldier went to a sage and asked: "Is there really a paradise to live for and a hell to avoid? I sincerely request you to favour me with a clear answer."*

*"Who are you?" asked the sage.*

*"I am a veteran soldier who has been honoured several times, but I am not satisfied. I am not fulfilled."*

*"You, a soldier!" exclaimed the sage, "who would give you the honours? You look more like a disappointed beggar."*

The soldier was so angry that he began to draw his sword, but the sage continued: "So you have a sword. Are you sure your weapon is sharp enough to cut off my head?"

As the soldier drew his sword in anger, the sage said, "Here open the gates of hell!"

At these words, the soldier, perceiving the sage's intention, sheathed his sword and bowed down, and sat at the feet of the sage.

"Here open the gates of paradise," observed the sage.

# FOUR

# The
# Sudden
# Awakening

'Being still and letting life flow' is the way a sage lives his life, or, is supposed to live his life. Perhaps more accurately, this is the way the sage sees his life being lived.

What the spiritual seeker has to understand – is that for the sage there is no separation between him and the 'others'. In actual life, however, it is clearly seen that the sage responds to his name being called; and, if we assume that a sage is not someone who lives as a recluse in a Himalayan cave but someone who lives his life as an ordinary citizen like any of us, then the sage, like any one of us, enjoys his pleasures and suffers the pains in the moment as a separate entity. In other words, the sage has to live his life as a separate entity, and therefore, necessarily must have an ego as separate from the 'others'.

The sage has to live his life as a separate entity – earning his livelihood, submitting his tax returns, having to face litigations – clearly separate from the 'others'. In other words, the sage has to live his life as a separate entity, which he cannot do unless he clearly sees his *separation* from the 'others'.

This situation has caused untold misery to the seekers through a basic confusion: does the sage have an ego or not? Does the sage not clearly see a separation between himself as a separate entity and the 'other' as another separate entity? And yet, the sage has always been expected not to see any separation between the 'me' and the 'other'! In other words, what is the basic difference between the sage and the 'me' who both have to live life as separate entities?!

It is an unfortunate fact that the books on *Advaita* and 'enlightenment' and similar subjects do not seem to address this problem. It is for this reason that we find spiritual seekers confessing, with tears in their eyes, that after thirty years of strict discipline and various spiritual practices, they have suddenly realised that there has not been any basic or essential change in their lives. They still find themselves having to face life from moment to moment, never knowing what pain the next moment may bring. They do not seem to ever feel anchored in peace and harmony while facing life from moment to moment. They still find themselves full of hatred: hatred for themselves for what they did to others, and hatred towards others for what they did to them – hatred that has been corroding their selves deep inside.

In what way is the sage different from me so that now, presumably, he is able to live his life anchored in peace and harmony? The sage is seen to be never uncomfortable with himself and never uncomfortable with others, while like me, he has to face the uncertainties of life from moment to moment. This would seem to be the focussed area in which the spiritual seeking should really be concentrating its attention.

There is also another area in which there is considerable confusion, which is based on the utterly mistaken belief that after 'enlightenment' the sage has suddenly become the perfect human being – without anger, without desire, without attachment, and so forth. And this mistaken belief is usually further encouraged by the hypocrisy of the fake gurus who assume the role of the perfect human being in their appearance, expressions, general behaviour, which is in studied contrast to the absolutely natural behaviour of the genuine sage who is not generally concerned about how the world sees him, and who has genuinely appreciated the great value of anonymity.

A seeker who has been corrupted by some fake gurus happens to be introduced to a genuine sage like Nisargadatta Maharaj, and the misguided seeker sees the supposed sage clearly showing his anger, enjoying his smoke, and showing obvious preference for certain foods. The seeker is greatly confused and can be forgiven if he comes to the conclusion that he should stay away from the genuine sage. But then that would be his destiny, according to the Will of God, according to the cosmic law.

The confusion on both counts is further confounded by the fact that the basic Ultimate Understanding can never really be put into words, and any such effort must necessarily cause considerable confusion, because any objective knowledge must necessarily be conceptual knowledge. It is a basic fact of all knowledge that the words used would be differently interpreted. This means that anything anyone has ever said, however sagely or saintly he may have been, must necessarily be a concept that would be acceptable to some and not acceptable to others. The truth must necessarily be that which no one can deny because that must be the experience of everyone. From this standpoint, the only Truth in life must be only One: I AM – the Impersonal Awareness of Being.

In objective science, anyone's understanding, assuming it is correct, would be perfectly valid for everyone else, and anyone could pass it on to others if it were adequately expressed. But the understanding of the One Reality – the Ultimate Understanding – is not of that kind, and it cannot be transferred or transmitted. All that can be done is to use language to point at it. No amount of description can replace the taste of a mango. This is the main difficulty in talking about the one Truth or One Reality. Phenomenally – that is, dualistically – all seeing means a subject seeing an object. But this knowledge of reality is not something to be seen because it is not an object. You could be led to within 'sight' of it but the 'seeing' would necessarily have to be done by you. Even this, unfortunately, can only be metaphorical because the Truth, not being objective, cannot be 'seen'. In other words, where the subjective Truth is concerned, no object – which is basically what the human being is – could ever, in a million years, 'see' it!

What am I trying to say? I am trying to say that it must necessarily be the 'ego' that is doing the spiritual seeking because an inert body can do nothing! What is the ego? An identification, brought about by divine hypnosis, with the body-mind organism as a separate entity, 'doing' whatever is happening through that organism: a reflection of the source or consciousness in the organism. Any seeing done by the ego as a separate entity can only be on the basis of a subject-object relationship: an object (as a subject) seeing another object. In other words, all phenomenal 'seeing' is based on two objects, each seeing the other object on a subject-object basis. What this clearly means is that, in fact, it is consciousness which really does the seeing through two body-mind instruments, with each entity considering itself the subject that sees the object.

What this means is that phenomenally – for all practical purposes – it is the ego-entity who is the seeker in the spiritual seeking: the ego seeking its source. And yet some Masters have said 'kill the ego'. Can one not imagine the horrendous confusion this has created? Is the ego being asked to commit *hara kiri*, to kill itself?! This is the issue that needs to be directly addressed. The sage has to live the rest of his life, after the enlightenment, as a separate entity in the same society, as he lived before; therefore, the ego has to remain as a separate entity so long as the body-mind organism is alive.

And yet, all the Masters cannot be wrong. Obviously what the Masters meant was that the sense of separation, denoted by the word 'ego', had to be annihilated before enlightenment could take place. In other words, while still functioning in life as a separate entity, it is obvious that the awakened sage does not see any effective separation between the separate ego-entities. Now we have a focal point on which to concentrate: how is it possible for a sage to live his life as a distinctly separate entity and yet feel no separation from the other ego-entities?

The only answer is that while the sage does live his life as a separate entity, responsible for his actions to the prevailing social regulations and legal provisions, his deepest possible understanding is that, in the words of the Buddha, "events happen, deeds are done, but there is no individual doer of any deed." In other words, the awakened sage has been able to accept, totally and absolutely, that each separate ego-entity is only a separate instrument, specially programmed, through which the Primal Energy produces, at any time and place, precisely that which is supposed to be produced, according to a conceptual cosmic law applicable to all eternity, all phenomenal manifestation. The energy works precisely like electricity functioning through all electrical gadgets, producing, through each gadget, precisely that which each gadget is designed to produce.

And it is a divine joke – perhaps a tragic one – that this principle of 'non-doership' is the basis of every religion. The *Bible* says: "Thy Will be done." Islam says: "*Inshah Allah*." The Hindu religion says: "Thou art the speaker, Thou art the listener; Thou art the doer, and Thou art the experiencer." And yet, we have had religious wars for centuries.

What we have to consider is: what is enlightenment, and what is this self-realisation supposed to do for the sage for the rest of his life that he did not have so far? self-realisation, according to my concept, is the absolute realisation that "events happen, deeds are done, but there is no individual doer of any deed," that all there is, is consciousness, functioning as Primal Energy and bringing about all events in manifestation; that it is consciousness witnessing the functioning of manifestation that is life as human beings know it, through the billions of sentient beings.

What has the sage got from the self-realisation? Peace and harmony as an anchor, while facing life from moment to moment. He did not have this peace and harmony earlier, because while facing life in the moment, all he did was to judge every happening as something done by someone and all the time blaming – and hating – someone, either himself or someone else. Therefore, earlier, what he was anchored in was guilt and shame for his own actions and hatred for the 'other's' actions. Peace and harmony were totally unknown; now, in the absence of guilt, shame, and hatred, he is never uncomfortable with himself, never uncomfortable with the 'other'.

While thus anchored in peace and harmony, how does the sage live his life? He lives his life witnessing life happening through the many body-mind organisms. While living happens – physical and mental activity through the body-mind organisms – he himself, as the ego *without the slightest semblance* of personal doership, remains still, watching life flowing through the many body-mind organisms, including his own. If someone asks him how he lives his life, his honest answer would be: Being still, 'letting life flow'.

If the sage is asked how he managed to get the total acceptance of non-doership, he will explain with utter humility: while he was investigating what seemed to him were his actions, he would come to the inevitable conclusion, every time, without exception, that if some event, over which he had no control, had not happened earlier, what he thought was his action would not have happened. If a thought had not happened, if he had not happened to see something, or hear something, or smell something, or taste something, or touch something –

something beyond his control – what he thought was his action would not have happened. And, during the course of his habitual investigation of his actions, somehow, at one time, a flash of total acceptance happened: "I *cannot* be the doer of any action; and, if I cannot be the doer of any action, no one else can, either." And that was *it*.

With this sudden awakening to the fact that the 'ego' is only an identification with a particular entity with a name and without any real freedom of choice and action, dawns a deeper understanding of a sense of brotherhood with the 'other' similar egos – all instruments, individually programmed, through which the Primal Energy functions to bring about whatever is supposed to happen according to the cosmic law. Then, there is no question of any competition between the various instruments, no question of any envy or jealousy. The programming in each human instrument – genes plus up-to-date conditioning in the relevant geographical and social environment – has also not been in the control of anyone.

One of the first things that happens with the sudden awakening is that the ego realises that its own programming contains a mixture of good and bad traits, positive and negative points. He himself is not perfect, and nor is anyone else. This realisation immediately brings about, along with the sense of brotherhood, a deep sense of tolerance for the human being – both himself and the 'other'.

Similarly, there happens the clear realisation that many words have lost their traditional interpretation. 'Love' used to mean an emotion experienced in certain clear personal channels, charged with possessiveness, shadowed by jealousy, with its counterpart 'hate' ever ready to take its place. Now, suddenly, 'love' does not seem to pass through personal channels: it seems more like 'pure' affectivity, a singularly purified kind of love. Suddenly, the terms 'divine love' and 'karma' have a very deep significance.

There is, moreover, a very clear recognition that, with the presence of this new transcendent awareness that arose with the demolition of the sense of personal doership, the love-hate relationship has given place to a purer affectivity, resembling compassion – benediction; excitement-distress has passed into serenity and tranquillity; and envy, fear, greed, and other forms of doer-polluted emotion are replaced by pure affectivity itself.

The awakened sage has also suddenly noticed that this new attitude to life – almost a fresh awareness – seems to be subject to a peculiar form of radiation which appears to attract others to him, apparently needing some kind of guidance, perhaps love.

The sage then finds himself facing life from moment to moment, accepting whatever the moment brings – sometimes pleasure, sometimes pain – but never uncomfortable with himself and never uncomfortable with others:  Being still, 'letting life flow'.

*The basic principle behind 'living happens' would be aptly illustrated by the story of the Sufi who was known in his neighbourhood as a saint who lived a pure life. Near him lived a pretty girl whose parents owned a store. Suddenly, without any warning, her parents discovered she was pregnant.  She would not confess who the father was, but after much harassment, named the Sufi. When they came to the Sufi in great anger and confronted him with their news, the Sufi took the news calmly and only said, "Is that so?"*

*After the child was born it was brought to the Sufi. By this time the Sufi had lost his reputation, which did not seem to bother him at all, but he took very good care of the baby.  He obtained milk from his neighbours and everything else the baby needed.  The neighbours, who knew the Sufi more intimately, knew that the girl was up to some mischief, and did their best to give every kind of help to the Sufi.*

*A year later, the young mother could stand it no longer, and told her parents the truth:  the real father was a handsome young man, working in the mechanic's shop close by.  The parents of the girl at once went to the Sufi, begged his pardon sincerely, and earnestly requested him to give them the one-year-old.  The Sufi gladly let them have the child, after a very loving goodbye.  All he said was, "Is that so?"*

# Anxiety
# in
# Life

It would seem from all outward appearances that our life is nothing but a spark of light between a series of tunnels of darkness. Nor is this interval between two nights an unclouded, sunny day, for between occasions of pleasure, we are vulnerable to pain.

There is the feeling that we live in a time of unusual insecurity. In the past several years so many long-established traditions have broken down – traditions of family and social life (now we are introduced not to a spouse but to a 'partner'), of economic order and of religious belief. As the years go by, we seem to find fewer and fewer things to hold on to, fewer things we can regard as right and true, and fixed for all time.

Human beings appear to be happy only so long as they seem to have a future they can look forward to. If happiness always depends on some expectation in the future, we are always chasing a will-o'-the-wisp that ever eludes our grasp, until eventually there is no more future to look forward to. In the best of times, 'security' has never been anything better than temporary and insubstantial, but one tries to make life more acceptable by belief in certain things beyond the reach of calamity – in God, in good government, in the eternal laws of basic right and goodness. Today, such convictions are rare, even in religious circles. It is quite clear that science has taken the place of religion in the popular imagination, and that scepticism has become more general than faith and belief in most things.

Nuclear physics and relativity have undoubtedly done away with the old materialism, but now we have a view of the universe with even less room to envisage any purpose and design in life. The scientists quite rightly argue that if you believe in God, you do so on purely emotional grounds, without any basis in logic or fact. It is really not atheism but agnosticism. It is of the essence of scientific method that you do not employ hypotheses that cannot be tested. But modern physicists, with the theory of uncertainty, seem to have arrived at a dead end: how did consciousness get into matter? But that is another matter altogether. Man seems to be unable to live without some sort of myth, without the belief that the routine and drudgery, the pain and fear of this life must have some meaning and good in the future.

When belief in the eternal becomes impossible, human beings seek their happiness in the joys of time.

However much they may try to bury it in the depths of their minds, they simply cannot be unaware that these joys are both uncertain and ephemeral. Consequently, our age is one of frustration, anxiety, agitation, and addiction to alcohol and drugs. We look for a higher standard of living, a violent and complex stimulation of the senses. We crave distraction: a panorama of sights, sounds, thrills and titillations into which we must crowd as much as possible in the shortest possible time. This is no exaggeration – it is the simple reality for millions of lives.

Is there not a way out of this impasse?

The common error of ordinary religious practice is to mistake the symbol for the reality, to look at the finger pointing out the way and then to suck it for comfort rather than follow the pointing. The words 'water' or 'fire' are useful for communication. The same is true of 'God'. The reality which is denoted by 'God' and 'eternal life' is truly honest, plain and above-board, and transparently open for all to see. But the seeing requires a correction in the mental approach, just as clear vision sometimes requires a correction in the eyes.

The believer will open his mind to the truth – or a concept – on condition that it fits in with his pre-conceived ideas and wishes. What is needed is 'faith'. Faith is an unreserved opening of the mind to the new concept, *whatever it may turn out to be*. Faith has no pre-conceptions: it is a plunge into the unknown; belief clings, faith lets go. Belief has become an attempt to hang on to life, to grasp, to keep it for one's own. But you really cannot grasp it, just as you cannot walk away with a river in a bucket. The same is true of 'life' and of 'God'.

We have never actually understood the revolutionary sense beneath the words regarding the basic tenets of almost every religion. Hence the many religious wars. The incredible truth is that what religion calls the 'vision of God' is found only in giving up any belief in a particular concept of God. We discover the 'Infinite' and the 'Absolute' not by straining to escape from the finite and relative world, but only by the most complete acceptance of its limitations. Likewise, we can find life meaningful only when we have truly seen that it is without any purpose according to any concept based on man's limited intellect, and we can know the 'mystery of the universe' only when we surrender our intellect and realise that we can know nothing at all about it.

The usual agnostic, relativist, or materialist fails to reach this point because he does not have the patience to follow his line of thought persistently to its end – an end which would be the surprise of his life. The discovery of the mystery – "the wonder and marvel of the magnificence of God's creation," as Meister Eckhart has put it – needs no belief because the basis of belief is what we have already known. But this is beyond any imagination. We have only to keep the eyes of the mind fully open, and "the truth will out."

# SIX

# Faith in God

It would seem that 'faith' is a combination of belief and trust, resulting in unshakeable acceptance. On this basis, there can never be a loss of faith. If I have faith in God, such faith cannot depend upon my interpretation of what happens. If my faith in God depends upon God doing whatever I want at any time, it really cannot be called 'faith' – it may be 'hope' in God. True faith in God can only mean my unshakeable acceptance of whatever happens at any time as something that could not have not happened at that time and place.

I want something that I know is not unjustified; I worked hard for something and I should get an adequate result. If I do get what I think I deserved, then is it an indication of my faith in God? If I do not get what I think I deserve, should I lose my faith in God? True faith in God can only be based on the absolute acceptance of the concept "Thy Will be done." If what I wanted did not happen, I can only interpret that it was not God's Will that I should get what I wanted at that time. But the more important content of my faith in God is the fact that I really cannot know whether what I wanted at the time was really good for me or not in the long run. Therefore, my faith in God enables me to accept whatever happens at any time as something that simply had to happen according to a cosmic law, the basis of which cannot ever be known by the mere mortal with his very limited knowledge and intellect. As Neils Bohr explained to Albert Einstein, "We think God plays dice with the universe because we do not have the full information which God has about the universe." In other words, the human intellect can envisage a very limited vision, while God's vision covers all space into eternity.

There are many agnostics whose 'no belief' is a rather vague proposition. But then, there are atheists who simply do not accept the principle of the existence of a God. What the atheists do not accept is a particular concept of God: God as a rigid taskmaster, an exaggerated version of one's boss, or an uncompromising moralist with an account book for noting down everybody's sins. Actually, there is nothing really blasphemous in the rejection of God because what they reject is an absurd concept of God.

It would be ridiculous not to accept the idea of 'God' as the One Source from which the entire manifestation has emerged. The alternative would be that the manifestation occurred as an accident. The result of an accidental creation would necessarily be chaos. But the universe as it exists is far from being chaotic. Therefore, the concept of an accidental creation would only be a matter of cussedness or perversion.

It is astonishing to what extent the concept of 'faith in God' can be corrupted. There is the story of a rabbi who prided himself on his faith in God:

*Once, there was a flood. The water was rising steadily. This man sat in his house, and when other people were leaving the area, they asked him to go with them, but he insisted on staying where he was, asserting his faith in God. The water kept rising, and a second boat came along, and the same thing happened. Finally, a helicopter came along, and he was told, "Look, this is your last chance. We'll throw you a rope. Climb up and get in; there will be no more help coming." The man refused, still asserting his faith in God. The waters kept rising and, of course, the man drowned. So when he met God in heaven, he asked Him, "I had implicit faith in you. Why did you let me drown?" God told him sternly, "Look, I tried three times to help you. I sent you a boat twice; I even sent you a helicopter."*

In actual practice, in daily living, faith in God is a beautiful concept. I know that life means 'doing'. Therefore, at any moment, I do whatever I think I should be doing, with the absolute faith that it is not me who is actually doing anything but that it is the Primal Energy, functioning through my body-mind organism, which

49

brings about whatever is to be brought about, according to God's Will, according to the cosmic law, together with the resulting consequences. No one can know what the actual result will be of any action. All that I can do is to do, at any moment, whatever I think I should do, and thereafter let God look after his creation, as Ramana Maharshi used to say.

In other words, all that anyone can do, at any moment, is to do whatever one thinks one should do, and thereafter, be still and 'let life flow'. And, 'being still' means doing whatever one needs to do in the present moment, without conceptualising about the past or the future.

# SEVEN

# Awareness
# and
# Silence

For four frozen months in the Antarctic winter of 1934, Admiral Byrd was engaged in the search for scientific data. One day, standing absolutely still on that icy no-man's land, he became intensely aware of the vast deep silence. Later that evening, he made a note in his diary:

> "In that instant of utter silence, the realisation dawned upon me that I was part of God, part of the universe and that I was not alone."

Admiral Byrd discovered, in that stillness, what can be discovered by any of us in the deep recesses of our own being, in the quiet of the early morning at home, in the brief moments of sincere prayer, while taking a walk in the park, or perhaps, even while waiting for an appointment at the dentist's waiting room! In absolute silence is always present an absolute power. Such silence, such stillness, of course, means a really vacant, empty mind.

Sri Aurobindo draws from his own experience in the poem *Savitri*:

"A stillness absolute, incommunicable
Meets the sheer self-discovery of the soul."

Generally, quietude, calmness, peace, silence, and stillness are assumed to be identical states of mind. But the mystic tells us that in reality this is not so. The various states are of a deepening order of consciousness, silence being the deepest. In a state of deep silence, there are no thoughts, feelings, or mental movements that can disturb or alter the peace of the inner-being. The human mind, in its emptiness, gets absorbed in the core of silence where it is able to touch the original source of Energy, Love, the Purity of Being, and discover the soul, our true self within. Here God becomes a living presence.

It is an unfortunate part of our modern urban existence that while silence is actually knocking at the door of our spirit, we seldom hear it because thousands of years of conditioning have made us fear the deep silence within us. And, curiously enough, the fact was sadly brought to my attention that this fear of silence pervades the mind of even a four-year-old child, when one morning, the neighbour's child came to our apartment to show something to me and my wife. My wife was in the bathroom, so I told the child that Auntie would be out very soon. At once, the four-year-old child promptly asked me: "What shall I do while I am waiting for Auntie?"

A good way of getting rid of this fear of silence and stillness is to start the practice of daily periods of meditation. To start with, even a period of fifteen or twenty minutes would be enough. Thereafter, it is the experience of most people that the mind, in course of time, begins to understand and appreciate the beauty of silence, and the period of meditation gradually extends itself. And soon, we find ourselves automatically clearing the debris of our usual routine affairs to make room for the regular period of meditation. Silence and meditation connect us with our inner-being-awareness – and, at the end of·daily meditation, we find ourselves re-entering the everyday world rejuvenated, with a fresh perspective.

Meditation makes us aware of the true nature of our being: silence and stillness, which we at one time were afraid to face. Silence and stillness does not necessarily mean absence of all sound. After a time, one becomes actually aware – silently – about a peculiar sound of silence, traditionally referred to as *naad*: a kind of humming *feeling*, rather than actual sound. And one then realises that in the depths of our being no one is separate from anything else. This is the union with the Divine.

## MYSTICAL NATURE OF SOUNDLESS SOUND

It is rather an interesting fact that soundless sound – *anaahat* – has been given considerable importance in almost all religions and faiths.

The *Bible* states: "In the beginning was the Word" (John 1.1). *Vedic* scriptures also affirm that the entire cosmic creation began with sound (*Brihadaranyaka Upanishad* 1.2.4). 'God is Word' indicates the physicality of sound but the concept of *nada* – that 'God is sound' – is more subtle because it is related to the Sanskrit word *nadi*, denoting the 'stream of consciousness'.

The concept of soundless sound – *ajapa* – is basically related to electrophysiology. Silent chanting generates a kind of energy that flows in a rhythmic wave pattern. Hans Berger, a German physicist, discovered that, in addition to the living tissues being sensitive to electric currents, the tissue itself, after a certain time, generated small voltages.

The audibility of sound waves depends on their frequency and velocity. A sound wave may be audible or inaudible, depending upon the medium through which it travels. All sound is the result of some sort of striking, and therefore, it has a beginning and an end. But if there could be a sound that is not struck, then it will have neither a beginning nor an end. Both heard and unheard, it will be imperishable.

A perfect example of soundless sound is given by Puran Singh in his book, *The Story of Ram*. Puran Singh arranged a series of lectures by Swami Ram Tirth in Japan which evoked tremendous response. Puran Singh, who authored Swami Ram Tirth's biography, writes:

"One night after dinner when Swami Ram Tirth went to sleep, around 12:30 at night he (Puran Singh) heard a feeble sound as though someone was saying 'Ram... Ram...'. Puran Singh opened the door but there was no one in the corridor. When he again heard the same sound, he entered the Swami's room, and found to his utter surprise, that though the Swami was fast asleep, the room was resounding with *Ram Naam* which was emanating from his body and not from his mouth."

According to the sage Ramana Maharshi, *japa*, when it becomes natural and automatic, is realisation; and *japa* may be done even when one is engaged in other work.

There is considerable power in the sacred word or sound. Steven J. Rosen, who wrote *The Hidden Glory of India*, says that a device called tonoscope graphically demonstrates the power of Sanskrit syllables to evoke form in a physical medium. The tonoscope is a tube suspended over a thin membrane covered by a layer of fine dust. When sounds are broadcast through the tube, corresponding designs form in the layer of dust that can tell us something about the initial sound that went through the tube. He says:

"While most sounds produce random ill-defined forms, the vibrations of Sanskrit syllables produce quite a different result. If the sounds of *mantras* can activate a gross element such as dust, one can only imagine the power such vibrations have on human consciousness."

The power of the spoken word, especially *japa*, has been described in other cultures also. Saint Paul has said, "Everyone who calls upon the name of the Lord will be saved" (*Romans* 10.15). Also, "From the rising of the sun to its setting the name of the Lord is to be praised," said King David (*Psalms* 113.3). The Buddha declared: "All who sincerely call upon my name will come to me after death and I will take them to paradise (*Vows of Amida Buddha* 18).

Be still, and you hear the soundless sound, when your thinking and conceptualising is totally absent. You can be doing your normal work and yet be still.

## MIND AND BREATH

Take a break from the mind. Follow the breath. The constant awareness of the breath will detach you from your mind. The energy that usually moves into thinking will move into witnessing.

Whenever you remember, be aware of your breathing. You may forget, but that's OK. The moment you remember, start being aware again. Sit silently; be aware of all that is happening around. You will soon be aware that your breath has been shallower, more rhythmic, bathing you in an inexplicable peace. Simply relax, do not 'try' to be aware. You are there, nothing to be done, everything is accepted, nothing is rejected.

Just be alert to the life energy that is moving within the body. No need to take a deep breath. If a deep breath happens, that is OK. Just be aware of the breath going out on its own, coming in on its own.

Steady awareness of your breathing will make your mind more steady, the functioning of your body more stable.

Deep silence, the door to understanding the What-Is is closed to those who are always craving for something, whatever it may be: fun or joy, or heaven or enlightenment. Truth is not a personal matter; the What-Is does not belong to anyone.

# EIGHT

# To Do
# or
# Not to Do

There is an inherent dilemma in the theory and practice of non-doership, which the human being simply cannot avoid. And this dilemma has got to be faced. This dilemma is, essentially, whether to watch life from the sidelines or to get involved, whether to decline or welcome responsibility – whether, in current slang, to cop out or not.

The spiritual theory does not make it easier to decide; if anything, it makes confusion worse confounded. Ramana Maharshi, for instance, says: "No one succeeds without effort; the successful few owe their success to their perseverance." And, yet, he also says: "A passenger in a train would be silly to keep his load on his head. Let him put it down; he will find that the load reaches the destination all the same." Similarly, let us not pose as the doers, but resign ourselves to the guiding power.

Then again, Jesus, in his *Sermon on the Mount*, tells

us to relax, to let tomorrow take care of itself, and leave everything to the hidden power that makes the lilies grow. At the same time, in the *Parable of the Talents*, he heaps praise on the busy, duty-bound, responsible citizen, and cheerfully consigns the unprofitable lay-about to hell!

The dilemma is really not a mere intellectual or theological puzzle. It is real and *it hurts*. As Douglas Harding has put it:

"Whether we take the way of just letting things happen, or the way of strenuous intervention, we are in for trouble. The life of the drop-out who exerts no effort and makes no decisions and accepts no responsibility for himself (let alone for his fellow-man) – what sort of a life is that? As for his opposite, the 'square' – the hard-working, conscientious, load-carrying public-spirited man – we all know the compromises and frustrations and anxieties that are coming to him, to say nothing of the decay and death that will shortly terminate himself and all his well-laid enterprises."

We obviously need a radical solution, a truly practical one that we can at once start to apply in our daily living. A simple way would be to find out how the sage has managed to witness the flow of life, without getting involved in it. Obviously, the sage is not a wilting, diluted, failed, irresponsible person. On the contrary, one finds the sage especially alive, and in his own way marvellously determined and energetic – and successful – in whatever he is doing in his daily life. In fact, one finds the sage the very opposite of those sad humans who seem to lack vital force. In other words, there is a world of difference between the dropout and the sage, no matter how alike their appearance and behaviour may happen to be!

And, wonder of wonders, the difference turns out to be simply in their attitude to life: the dropout considers himself a person who has apparently chosen to be a dropout for some reason that he cannot fathom; whereas the sage has come to the very firm, undoubted conclusion that he is not a person at all.

However, the seer has to spend the rest of his life in a society which does not accept the concept of non-doership.

This is what Ramana Maharshi has to say:
"Action forms no bondage. Bondage is only the false notion: 'I am the doer'... Be fixed in the Self and act according to nature without the sense of doership... Attending to the Self includes attending to the work ... The work will not bind you. It will go on automatically."

This is the key to the situation. According to my perception, the sage lives his life with the absolute, total conviction that no one is the doer, neither himself nor the 'other'. So far as his responsibility to himself is concerned, he is totally free of the bondage of guilt and shame that would be based on his being the doer; he would also be free of the bondage of hatred and malice, and envy and jealousy towards the 'other' for the latter's actions. In other words, the sage faces life from moment to moment, accepting whatever the moment brings – pain or pleasure – as being his destiny or the Will of God, according to a cosmic law, the basis of which no human being could ever possibly understand. At the same time, while facing life from moment to moment, the sage is firmly anchored in peace and harmony and tranquillity, never uncomfortable with himself, never uncomfortable with the 'other'.

The sage is never unaware of the fact that he has to continue to live his life in a society that does not generally accept the concept of non-doership, and continues to hold each individual entity responsible for his or her actions. This presents no problem to the sage. He accepts any action happening through his own body-mind organism as depending entirely on his own destiny (as the Will of God, according to a cosmic law). And, more important, he also accepts the judgement of society on 'his' action – good, bad or indifferent – as the Will of God.

In other words, the sage has been able to accept totally, absolutely, unconditionally, the concept of the Buddha, "events happen, deeds are done, but there is no individual doer of any deed." The sage, therefore, does live his life as a separate entity, responsible to society for his actions, with the firm understanding that all separate entities are, in fact, separate body-mind instruments through each of which it is the Primal Energy which functions and brings about the event or deed precisely according to the cosmic law.

What this all amounts to is that the sage lives his life, perfectly content to do whatever his 'nature' expects him to do, accepting whatever happens thereafter as God's Will. The sage lives his life, knowing that his life is being lived, and therefore, without any expectations of any kind.

If the sage is asked to say, very briefly, how he lives from day to day, his answer is likely to be: I remain still and watch life flow.

NINE

# Pain
# and
# Pleasure

At some time or the other, every one of us must have envied the animal that lives, suffers, enjoys life, and dies without making a 'problem' of it. Their lives seem to be so simple, uncomplicated. Their secret is that they are so busy doing whatever they are doing in the moment, that it never enters their heads to ask whether they are having fun, or whether life has a meaning. For the human being, happiness consists in not only enjoying life in the present moment, but in the assurance that there is a whole foreseeable future of joys ahead of him.

The human brain is unquestionably much more sensitive than that of the animal and, of course, this fact adds immensely to the richness of life. And yet, we pay dearly for this special prerogative because the very increase in sensitivity makes us peculiarly vulnerable to intense pains. Sensitivity requires a high degree of softness and fragility: the eyeballs, eardrums, taste buds, and nerve ends are not only soft and fragile but also perishable.

If we want intense pleasure, we cannot avoid intense pain. Indeed, it would seem that the two must in some way alternate, for continuous pleasure is a stimulus that must either pale or be increased. A consistent diet of rich food either destroys the appetite or makes for illness.

It is precisely because we are not willing to suffer for our pleasures, that the life we live is a contradiction and a conflict. The greater part of human activity is designed to make permanent those joys and experiences which are lovable only because they are changing. Music is a delight because of its rhythm and flow – the moment you arrest the flow and prolong a note or chord beyond its time, the rhythm is destroyed. To work for the exclusion of change is to work against the very basis of life.

The real problem of life does not come from any momentary sensitivity to pain, but from our consciousness of time and duration. The object of dread is, very often, not an operation in the immediate future. It is usually the problem of next month's rent, of a threatened war or social disaster, or of old age and death. The dread may, indeed, arise out of something in the past. The power of memories and expectations is such that the past and the future are more real than the present. The present joy can almost be nullified by the dread of the future.

If, in order to enjoy the enjoyable present, we have to have the assurance of a happy future, we are indeed 'crying for the moon'. No one can have any such assurance.

What is necessary, therefore, is to research, in depth, what it is that the human being is really searching for! Obviously, he is searching for that with which he can be anchored, so that life as it happens could be appreciated together with both pain and pleasure. And that could be termed 'peace'.

The persistence and changefulness of the world are the very core of its liveliness and loveliness. To be passing is to live; to remain and continue is to die: "Unless a grain of corn falls into the ground and dies, it remains alone. But if it dies, it brings forth much fruit." Movement and rhythm are of the essence of all things loveable. Every form is really a pattern of hidden movement, and every living thing is like the river, which, if it did not flow out, would never have been able to flow in.

Life and death are not two opposing forces; they are only two ways of looking at the same force, for the movement of change is as much the builder as the destroyer. The human body lives because it is a complex of motions, of circulation, of respiration, and digestion. To resist change, to try to cling to life, is therefore like holding your breath – if you persist you will kill yourself. When we fail to see that our life is change, we set ourselves against ourselves and become like Ouroboros, the misguided snake who tries to eat his own tail. Ouroboros is the perennial symbol of all vicious circles, of every attempt to split our being asunder and make one part conquer the other. The beautiful and the ugly, the good and the evil, the polaric interconnected opposites are the very essence of the manifestation and its functioning that we call 'life'.

In the great stream of life, specialisation in verbiage, classification, differentiation, and mechanised thinking has put man out of touch with many of the marvellous powers of 'instinct' that govern the body. It has, furthermore, made him feel utterly separate from the universe. And then, when all philosophy has dissolved in relativism, and can make fixed sense of the universe no longer, the isolated 'I' feels miserably insecure and always in panic, finding the real world a flat contradiction of its whole being.

This predicament is now social rather than individual; it is widely felt, not confined to just a few. Almost every spiritual tradition recognises that a point comes when two things have to happen: one, man must surrender his separate-feeling 'I'; and two, he must face the fact that he cannot ever know or define the Ultimate. Those traditions also recognise that beyond this point there remains a 'vision of God' that simply defies its being put into words. They also indicate that this vision is a restoration of something which we all had at one time and which we lost because we were not able to appreciate and accept it. This vision, then, is the "unclouded awareness of this indefinable 'something' which we call life, present reality, the great stream, the eternal now – an awareness without the sense of separation from it."

The moment I name it, it is no longer God: it may be man, tree, green, soft or hard, long or short, atom, universe.

Therefore, that ultimate something which cannot be defined or measured, may be represented by the word 'God'. This can truly only mean *that we cannot not know God all the time* – except when we begin to 'think' about it. This would remind me of St. Augustine's answer to the question, "What is time?": "I know, but when you ask me I don't." Yet, religion tells us that 'God' is someone (or something) from whom one can seek true wisdom and guidance. In fact, this kind of wisdom put in the form of specific directions, amounts to very little.

It was not through statements that we learned how to breathe, swallow, see, circulate the blood, digest food, or resist disease. Yet these things are performed by the most complex and marvellous processes that no amount of book learning and technical skill can replicate. This is real wisdom, but our brains have little to do with it. Without any technical apparatus or calculations for prediction, homing pigeons can return to their roosts from long distances away, migrant birds can revisit the same locations year after year, and plants can 'devise' extraordinary contraptions for disseminating their seeds in the wind. If they could talk, they could no more explain how it is done than man can explain how his heart beats.

We have been taught to neglect, despise, and violate our own bodies, and to put all faith in our brains. Indeed, the special disease of civilised man might be described as a block – or schism – between his brain (the cortex) and the rest of his body. In 'medical' language, it means we have allowed brain thinking to develop and dominate our lives out of all proportion to 'instinctual wisdom' which is being allowed to slump into atrophy. Thus, in one way or another, civilised man agrees with St. Francis in thinking of the body as 'Brother Ass'. But even theologians have recognised that the source of evil and stupidity lies not in the physical organism as a whole, but in the cut-off, dissociated brain, which they term the 'will'.

Human desire tends to be insatiable. We stimulate our sense organs until they become insensitive, so that if pleasure is to continue they must have stronger and stronger stimulants. In self-defence, the body gets ill from the strain, but the brain goes on and on. The brain knows that the future is limited, so that it must crowd all the pleasures of paradise and eternity into the span of a few years.

The 'primary consciousness' – the basic mind that knows reality rather than ideas about it, does not know the future. It lives completely in the present, and perceives nothing more than What-Is in the present moment. The ingenious 'brain', however, looks into memory and makes predictions that make the future assume such a high degree of reality that the present moment loses its value.

Thus, the 'brainy' economy designed to produce happiness, not of solid and substantial realities but abstract and superficial things like promises, hopes, and assurances, is a fantastic vicious circle which must produce more and more pleasures, or collapse!

The brain is clever enough to see the vicious circle that it has made for itself. But it can do nothing about it. Seeing that it is unreasonable to worry does not stop worrying – you worry all the more. Neither side actually wants a war, and yet, because we live in a vicious circle, we start the war to prevent the other side from starting it first and gaining an advantage. From this rational point of view, we find ourselves in the dilemma of St. Paul: "To will is present with me; but how to perform that which is good I find not. For the good that I would I do not." But the fact of the matter is not that the will or 'spirit' is reasonable and the flesh perverse, but that the whole organism is 'a house divided against itself' which cannot stand; the whole organism is perverse because the brain is divided against the belly, and the head unconscious of its union with the tail.

The realisation must happen that the function of the brain is to serve the present moment – the real – and not to send man chasing wildly after the phantom of the non-existing future. Working rightly, the brain is the highest form of 'instinctual wisdom'. Thus, it should work like the homing instinct of pigeons and the formation of the foetus in the womb – without verbalising the process or knowing 'how' this is done. The self-conscious brain, like the self-conscious heart, is a disorder, and manifests itself in the acute feeling of separation between 'I' and my experience.

The brain can only assume its proper behaviour when there is the realisation that consciousness is doing what it is supposed to do: not writhing and whirling to get out of the present experience, but being effortlessly aware of it. It is only the horizontal thinking in duration that keeps the brain from not being aware of it.

# TEN

# On
# Being
# Aware

Now we have created a problem for ourselves: How are we to heal the split between 'I' and 'me', the brain and the body, man and nature, and bring to an end all the vicious circles which it produces? How are we to experience life as something other than as a honey trap in which we are the struggling bees? How are we to find security and peace of mind in a world whose very nature is insecurity, unceasing change, and impermanence? All these questions, demanding a method and course of action, show that the problem itself has not been understood: we do not need action – yet. We need more light – light means awareness: to be aware of life, of experience as it is in the moment, without any concepts, ideas, or judgements about it.

The truth is revealed by removing things that stand in the way, an art, not unlike sculpture, wherein the artist creates not by building but by hacking away that portion which prevents the final vision from being seen.

There is a basic contradiction in wanting to be perfectly secure in a universe whose very nature is fluidity and change. But the contradiction lies deeper: to be secure means to isolate and fortify the 'I', but it is precisely this feeling of being isolated that makes me feel lonely and afraid. Thus, the desire for security and the feeling of insecurity are the same thing. This is the crux of the problem: to stand face to face with insecurity is still not to understand it. To understand the problem, we must not just face it – we have to be it.

The notion of security is based on the feeling that there is something within ourselves that is permanent which endures through all the changes of life. It is for this enduring core – which we call 'me' – that we are struggling for security. This 'me' is considered the real 'I' – the thinker of our thoughts, the feeler of our feelings, the knower of our knowledge. All that is necessary is for us to realise the utter non-existence of this illusory 'me'. Understanding can come only through awareness. Can we then approach our experience quite simply, as if we had never known it before, and, without prejudice, look at what is going on?

The fact of the matter is that there is, in any moment, only the experience, never the individual experiencer. It is for this reason that you cannot compare this present experience with any past experience. You can only compare it with a memory of the past, which is a part of the present experience. When it is clearly seen that it is indeed a form of present experience, then it will also be as clearly seen that trying to separate yourself from this experience – as the experiencer – is as impossible as trying to make your teeth bite themselves or to make your eyes see themselves. There is, simply, experience – not someone experiencing an experience.

In other words, any separate 'I', who thinks thoughts and experiences an experience, is utterly an illusion. To understand this is to realise that life is entirely momentary – from moment to moment – that there is neither permanence nor security, that there is no 'I' to be protected. What-Is is the present moment. To understand this moment I must try not to be divided from it. I must be aware of the present moment with my whole being. Actually, it is the only thing I can do. Everything else is the insanity of attempting the impossible.

To understand joy or fear, one has to be wholly and undividedly aware of it. This surely, is the meaning of that strange saying: "If thine eye be single, thy whole body shall be full of light." In other words, be still.


AN AMAZING MOMENT

If one were suddenly asked, "At this moment, who are you?" there can really be no answer. If one stops to think, one would give information about one's name, address, business etc., but that would be about the past, not about the present moment. To be aware of reality, of the living present, is to discover that, at each moment, the experience is all. There can be nothing else besides it – no experience of any 'me' experiencing the experience.

It is a curious fact that we are usually ready enough to be aware of the moment in times of happiness and pleasure, and to 'forget ourselves'. But with the arrival of the pain, whether physical or emotional, whether actual or anticipated, the mind divides itself from itself, to be separate from the experience. The human organism has wonderful powers of adaptation to both physical and psychological pain, but only when the pain is not being constantly re-stimulated by the inner effort to get away and escape from it, to separate the 'me' from the feeling. It is not an uncommon fact that quite a few older people have some ache or pain somewhere in the body most of the time, but seem to be able to live with it until someone reminds them of it!

The point is that when we try to understand the present by comparing it with memories (when we did not have the pain), we cannot understand it as deeply as when we are aware of it without comparison. As we cannot get out of the present, our only escape is into past memories. But the fact is that memories cannot get one away. And this is not all. The more we accustom ourselves to understanding the present in terms of past memory, the unknown by the known, the more joyless and frustrated life becomes. On the other hand, being totally aware of it with our whole being is a new experience: we do not resist, and the whole conflict between the 'me' and the present moment vanishes. We merely witness whatever the body does – perhaps even scream.

In other words, the answer to pain is neither careless drifting nor fearful clinging to the past, but in being completely sensitive to each moment, in having the mind open and wholly receptive. This truly is not a theory but an actual experiment: a concept, the truth of which can only be tested in one's own experience. If, when swimming, you are caught in a strong current, it is fatal to resist; you must swim with it and gradually edge to the side.

Seeing that there is no escape from the pain, the mind yields to it, absorbs it, and becomes conscious of just pain without any 'me' feeling it or resisting it. In other words, the mind experiences pain in the same total, unselfconscious way in which it experiences pleasure. Sometimes, when resistance ceases, the pain simply goes away or dwindles to a bearable ache. The pain may remain but is no longer a problem. Wanting to get away from the pain is the real pain. When you become the pain, it ceases to be a cause of something. It hurts – that's it.

The real point is that this is not an experiment to be held in reserve, like a trick to be used against someone you do not like, for moments of crisis. It has to be a way of life. Let life flow. It means being aware, alert, sensitive to the present moment always, in all actions and relations, from now on. Another point that must be made clear is that accepting the pain means just witnessing every aspect of the pain, including the reaction of the body: the body may scream in pain – this is also witnessed and not suppressed. Jesus Christ, on the cross, screamed out, "Father, why have you abandoned me?" Ramakrishna Paramahamsa screamed out in pain, "Mother, why are you torturing me like this?" But then, the deep understanding and acceptance provided the answer, "Thy Will be done." What is the point in resisting the inevitable? The key is understanding. To ask how to do this, or seek a method or technique, is to miss the point altogether. One must realise that 'the mystery of life is not a problem to be solved but a reality to be experienced'.

What is important is the present moment. We learn nothing of much importance if it can be explained entirely in terms of past experience. If it were possible to understand all things in terms of what we know already, we could convey the sense of colour to a blind man with nothing but sound, taste, touch, and smell. It is absurd to seek God in terms of a preconceived idea of what God is. To believe in God, and to look for the God you believe in, is simply to seek confirmation of an opinion or concept. Is it not making a mockery of your seeking, to ask for a revelation of God's Will, and then to 'test' it by reference to your preconceived moral standards? You create a 'God', give him various attributes like all-knowing, all-merciful, and others, and then ask Him, "O Lord, Why do you create handicapped children?!"

Life and living cannot be lost in past and future. Life is alive, vivid, and vibrant in the present moment, containing depths that we have hardly begun to explore. The mind cannot divide itself into 'me' and the experience of the moment. The moment is all that you are and all that you know: "In this house there is no room for thee and me." In any experience in the moment, there is no room for thee and me.

# ELEVEN

# Poverty
# and
# Prosperity

A statement like "Thy Will be done" needs absolutely no explanation or interpretation to understand it. The meaning is quite clear: nothing can happen unless it is the Will of God; therefore, whatever is at this moment is the Will of God. But a statement to the effect that it would be easier for a camel to go through the eye of the needle than for a rich man to enter the Kingdom of God would certainly seem to need an explanation. Does it mean then that a sage King like Janaka could never have been an enlightened sage? Would a rich man who has inherited his wealth – and not earned it by dubious means – have to give up his wealth before he could hope for spiritual grace? And then, of course, what exactly is 'poverty'? To be below the subsistence level or the poverty line, to be in a situation where one does not know where the next meal is going to come from?

I would be inclined to seek the middle course: not to be either filthy rich or below the poverty level, to be

reasonably comfortable in life, to be in a frame of mind
to think about salvation, enlightenment, self-realisation
– peace of mind. It would not be difficult at all for me to
accept totally that the spiritual quality in the human being
would seem to exist in inverse ratio to acquired material
prosperity. In parts of the world where poverty prevails
much more widely than prosperity, the spiritual quality is
more likely to be found than in parts of the world in which
material prosperity has been imposed on the population. It
seems unlikely that material prosperity – a higher standard
of living – could have a substantial bearing on the spiritual
quality of life: what might be called 'happiness' – peace
of mind, harmony, contentment.

Indeed, research led by London School of Economics
professors into the link between personal spending
power and the perceived quality of life conclusively
proved that money can buy everything but happiness.
The study revealed that people in Bangladesh, one of
the poorest countries in the world, derived far more
happiness from their small incomes than, for example,
the British (thirty-second on the list) did from their
relatively large bank balances. The United States
ranked only forty-sixth in this World Happiness Survey.
This study showed that a link still existed, in the
poorer countries, between money and happiness,
because a small increase in income could mean vast
improvements in the basic necessities of life. However,
beyond a certain income level, that direct relationship
broke down, and it was found that happiness in rich

countries was far more dependent on close personal relationships, good health, and job satisfaction.

It seems clear, therefore, that more and more material prosperity, as an aim in life, can have no spiritual significance. On the other hand, poverty has positive value in the eyes of men such as St. Francis of Assisi, and material prosperity a negative value.

It seems quite unlikely, however, that the *attainment* of poverty could have any greater significance than the *attainment* of prosperity. Would it not, therefore, seem reasonable that the material condition of a man, like the shape of his nose, or his height and weight, may as well remain as what he was born with, as part of his normal programming and design on the plane of manifestation?

There is also one other point: Those who think in terms of material prosperity – the 'Materialists' – always seem to be thinking in terms of 'rights' rather than 'duties'. And yet it has been proved, time and again, that it is the performance of duties – job satisfaction – rather than the exercise of rights that produces peace of mind, contentment, serenity, and happiness. Why? As Wei Wu Wei has put it: "Perhaps because willingly to serve is a Positive action, to exact service a Negative action. But the acceptance of willing service is Positive, just as the performance of exacted service is Negative. Therein lies an adequate explanation of the misery of much that is contemporary life."

# TWELVE

# Living Happens
## and Includes
### the 'Me'

It is not easily acceptable, but the fact is that all the qualities that we admire or loathe in the world around us are reflections from within – our genes and our conditioning constituting our 'programming' – though from a within that is also a beyond, unconscious, vast, unknown. As one psychologist has put it: "Our feelings about the crawling world of the wasps' nest and the snake pit are feelings about hidden aspects of our own bodies and brains, and of all their potentialities for unfamiliar creeps and shivers, for unsightly diseases and unimaginable pains."

Again, it is not easy to accept it, but the fact is that the feeling that we stand face-to-face with the world, cut off and set apart, has a great deal of influence on thought and action. This has a great influence on our 'vision of life' – understanding of life as it is, of what we are, and what we are doing. Full awareness of the moment brings about a healed vision of life: it involves a deep transformation of our view of the world in knowing and feeling that the world is an organic unity. This has always been the view of the mystic, but the physicist is just now reluctantly being brought to this viewpoint.

It is a fact that most people feel separate from everything that surrounds them. Nevertheless, the physical reality is that my body exists only in relation to this universe, and I am as attached to it and dependent on it as a leaf on a tree. I feel cut off only because I am split within myself: I try to be separate from my own feelings and sensations. When I become aware of the unreality of this division – the 'me' is truly only a thought – the universe does not seem foreign any more. I cease to feel isolated when I recognise that I do not 'have' a sensation of the sky – there is the sensation and I am that sensation.

To discover that the many are the One and that the One is the many – the sense of unity with the 'All' – is to realise that both are words and noises representing what is indeed obvious to sense and feeling, an enigma to logic and description. Horizontal thinking in duration – the separation from the moment – is what brings about the separation of the 'me' from the rest of the world.

*A young seeker in search of spiritual wisdom was accepted by a Master as a disciple. The sage made him his personal attendant. After a few months, the young man*

*complained that thus far he had received no instruction.
The sage was genuinely astonished. "What do you
mean?" said the sage. "When you brought me my rice did
I not eat it? When you brought me my tea, did I not
drink it? When you made salutations to me, did
I not return the salutations? When have I ever
neglected to give you instruction?" When the young
man was totally mystified, the sage explained, "When
you want to see into anything, see into it directly. When
you begin to think about it, you miss it altogether."*

"Plucking chrysanthemums along the East fence;
Gazing in silence at the southern hills;
The birds flying home in pairs
Through the soft mountain air of dusk –
In these things there is a deep meaning,
But when we are about to express it,
We suddenly forget the words."

"The meaning is not the contemplative twilight
and perhaps, superficially idyllic atmosphere beloved of
Chinese poets. This is already expressed, and the poet
does not gild the lily," says Alan Watts. "He will not,
like so many Western poets, turn philosopher and say
that he is 'one with' the flowers, the fence, the hills
and the birds. This too is gilding the lily, or in his own
Oriental idiom, 'putting legs on the snake'. For when
you really understand that you are what you see and
know, you do not run around the countryside thinking,
'I am all this'. There is simply, 'all this'."

To know reality, you cannot stand outside it and define it; you can only enter into it, feel it, BE it. Otherwise, like everything else that the divided mind of subject-object creates, it would be a vicious circle. On the other hand, the realisation that the mind is actually undivided must have a corresponding, far-reaching influence on thought and action.

The divided mind comes to the dinner table, peeks at one dish after another, comparing with the earlier meals, and finds nothing good because there is nothing which it has fully tasted. On the other hand the sage, with an undivided mind, is known as a super-enjoyer (*Maha bhokta*) because for him, he is indeed this moment now; he is relaxed and tastes the pleasure to the full – or the pain, from which he does not try to escape. Then the sage has realised why this universe exists with its inevitable interdependent counterparts. The entire problem of justifying nature, of trying to make life mean something in terms of the future, totally disappears.

The meaning and purpose of the dancing is the dance itself, not that you are pursuing something. Like music, it is fulfilled in each moment. You do not play a sonata *in order* to reach the final chord: "Beethoven, Brahms, and Wagner were particularly guilty of working up to colossal climaxes and conclusions, and then blasting away at the same chord, over and over again, engaging the moment by being reluctant to leave it."

To the undivided mind of the sage, death is another moment, which cannot yield its secret unless lived to the full. Death is the unknown in which we lived before birth. Nothing is more creative than death: it is the whole secret of life. It means that the past must be abandoned, that the unknown cannot be avoided, that the 'me' cannot continue for all time. When a man truly accepts this without any doubt at all, he lives truly for the first time in his life. As Goethe has put it: "As long as you do not know how to die and come to life again, you are but a sorry traveller on this dark earth."

# THIRTEEN

# Freedom
## in
### Living

If we expect man to change his way of life, from the viewpoint of morality, we must assume that he is free to do so, for if he is not, nothing will make any difference; on the other hand, if he is acting under some compulsion, he is not making a free act. If a man is not free, threats and promises may modify his conduct, but there cannot be any essential change. If he is free, threats and promises will not make him use his freedom.

The meaning of true freedom cannot be grasped by the divided mind. Freedom will seem to be the extent to which I can push the world about and fate the extent to which I get pushed around by the world. But to the whole mind – there is no 'me' other than the experience in the present moment – there is no contrast of 'me' and the world. There is just one Primal Energy functioning according to a cosmic law, and it does everything that happens. It raises my little finger and it creates earthquakes. We are accustomed to think of freedom as the separate human will and its power of choice.

What we ordinarily mean by choice is not real freedom. Choices are usually decisions motivated by pleasure and pain. But the best pleasures, according to everyone's personal experience, happen to be those for which we had not planned; and the worst part of pain is expecting it and trying to get away from it. One is assured by doctors that under certain circumstances, death can be a highly pleasant experience.

Actually, the sense of not being free comes from trying to do things that are either impossible or meaningless. You are not 'free' to draw a square circle or to stop certain reflex actions. Then again, the theory that we must inevitably do what gives us the greater pleasure or the lesser pain, is really a meaningless assertion based on verbal confusion: whatever we desire is pleasure!

The fact of the matter is that there really cannot be any question of freedom so long as the mind believes in the possibility of escape from What-Is in this moment. It may sound like abject fatalism to admit that What-Is in the moment could not have been anything else. It may seem that if I am afraid, then I am 'stuck' with fear, but in fact, I am chained to the fear only so long as I am trying to get away from it. When, on the other hand, I accept the fact without calling it 'fear', 'bad', or 'negative', it changes instantly into something else and life moves ahead. The feeling does not perpetuate itself if it does not get any sustenance from the feeler behind it.

The opposite of fear may be considered the feeling of 'love'. St. Augustine described it as: "Love, and do what you will." But the problem is how to love what you do not like. There is no formula for generating the authentic warmth of love. You cannot talk yourself into it. In any case, it would not be authentic. Everyone has love, but it can only come out when one is convinced of the frustration arising out of the impossibility of trying to love oneself. This conviction will not come through condemnations, through hating oneself, through calling self-love all the bad names in the universe. It can come only in the awareness that there is, truly, no self to love or hate, through the awareness that all that seems like actions are only happenings, and not the doing by anyone.

The present moment is the "door of heaven," the "straight and narrow way that leadeth into life." The rich man who carries too much baggage of the past and the future cannot get through this door.

That the eternal life can only be understood in this sense of the present moment is beautifully expressed by Meister Eckhart:

"The Now-moment in which God made the first man and the Now-moment in which the last man will disappear, and the Now-moment in which I am speaking are all one in God, in whom there is only one Now. Look! The person who lives in the light of God is conscious neither of time past nor of time to come but only of one eternity... Therefore he gets nothing new out of future events, nor from chance, for he lives in the Now-moment that is, unfailingly, 'in verdure newly clad'."

We are living in a time when human knowledge has gone so far that it begins to be at a loss for words: "The dust on the shelves has become as much of a mystery as the remotest stars." The physicist Eddington is nearest to the mystics when he says, quite simply, "Something unknown is doing we don't know what" – and, we may add, or why!

As Alan Watts has concluded:
"Discovering this the mind becomes whole: the split between I and me, man and the world, the ideal and the real, comes to an end. Paranoia, the mind beside itself, becomes *metanoia*, the mind with itself and so free from itself."

With this total understanding, the sage lives his life, from moment to moment, eating something when he is hungry, drinking something when he is thirsty, laughing whole-heartedly when he is amused (perhaps at something he is supposed to have done). So while 'living', he is ready to 'die' any moment – never uncomfortable with himself, never uncomfortable with others. The sage is always still, watching life flow.

# FOURTEEN

# Life Happens –
# Living Happens

It is an astonishingly refreshing experience to listen totally to the record of Lin-chi's teaching – *Lin-chi Lu* – which shows a character of immense vitality and awesome originality, talking to his students in informal and often somewhat 'racy' language.

Again and again, he berates them for not having enough faith in nature, for letting their minds "gallop around," in search of something that they have never lost, and which is "right before you at this very moment." Awakening, for Lin-chi, seems essentially a matter of 'nerve' – the strength and courage to 'let go' without further delay in the unwavering faith that one's natural spontaneous functioning is the Buddha mind.

*One is reminded, at this stage, of the story of a man wandering around the plateau on a mountain, who suddenly finds himself hanging on to the edge of a cliff. He knows there is no one else on the plateau, but cannot restrain himself from shouting for help. Suddenly, he hears a voice saying, "Yes, I am here and I can help, you but you must do exactly what I say." The unfortunate man immediately agrees to do whatever he is instructed to do. Continues the voice, "Alright. Now, let go of your grip." For a few seconds, there is no response from the man. Finally, he shouts: "Is anyone else up there?"*

To get back to Lin-chi, he was asked why he talks at all when he knows that the seeker is seeking something he has never lost. Says Lin-chi:

"Why do I talk here? Only because you followers of the Tao go galloping around in search of the mind, and are unable to stop it. On the other hand, the ancients acted in a leisurely way, appropriate to circumstances (as they happened). O, you followers of the Tao – when you get any point of view you will sit in judgement on top of the Buddha's head. Those who have completed the ten states will seem like underlings, and those who have arrived at Supreme Awakening will seem as if they had cangues around their necks. The *Arhaus* and *Pratyaka* Buddhas are like a deity privy. *Bodhi* and *nirvana* are like hitching-posts for a donkey."

On the importance of the 'natural' or 'unaffected' life and living, he is especially emphatic:

"There is no place in Buddhism for using effort. Just be ordinary and nothing special. Relieve your bowels, pass water, put on your clothes, and eat your food. When you are tired, go and lie down. Ignorant people may laugh at me, but the wise will understand. As you go from place to place, if you regard each one as your own home they will all be genuine, for when circumstances come you must not try to change them. Thus your usual habits of feeling, which make *karma* for the Five Hells, will of themselves become the Great Ocean of Liberation."

Then again, on the seeking of liberation itself creating *karma*:

"Outside the mind there is no *Dharma*, and inside also there is nothing to be grasped. What is it that you seek? You say on all sides that the Tao is to be practiced and put to the proof. Do not be mistaken. If there is anyone who can practice it, this is entirely *karma* making for birth-and-death. You talk about being perfectly disciplined in your six senses and in the thousand ways of conduct, but as I see it all this is creating *karma*. To seek the Buddha and to seek the *Dharma* is precisely making *karma* for the hells."

The genuine Zen flavour exists when a man is almost miraculously natural *without intending to be so*. His Zen life is not to make himself but to *grow* that way. In other words, the 'naturalness' of Zen flourishes only when one has lost affectedness and self-consciousness of any description. But a spirit of this kind comes and goes like the wind, and is the most difficult thing to institutionalise and preserve.

The characteristic most expressed would then seem to be the immediate or instantaneous awakening without having to pass through preparatory stages of various kinds of discipline. In other words, if *nirvana* is actually here and now, then to seek it is to lose it; one would have to see into it in the present moment, directly: a flash of direct understanding has to happen.

So listen to Saraha:
"If it (the Truth) is already manifest, what's the use of meditation? And if it is hidden, one is just measuring darkness. *Mantras* and *tantras*, meditation and concentration, they are all a cause of self-deception. Do not defile in contemplation thought that is pure in its own nature, but aid in the bliss of yourself and cease those torments... The nature of the sky is originally clear, but by gazing and gazing the sight becomes obscured."

Then again, the Six Precepts of Tilopa:
"No thought, no reflection, no analysis,
No cultivation, no intention;
Let it settle itself."

Immediate release without any special contrivance or intention is also implied in the idea of *sahaja*, the 'easy' or 'natural' state of the liberated sage.

A special point to be noted in all these pronouncements is that awakening was all too consistent with the affairs of daily living, and that, indeed, the highest attainment was to 'enter' into awakening without exterminating the 'defilements' of daily living. However, not exterminating the passions does not mean letting them flourish untamed. It means letting go of them rather than fighting them, neither suppressing passion nor indulging it. The idea clearly is to achieve it by non-interference (*wu-wei*), a kind of psychological judo.

The whole point of all seeking is to discover the self in oneself, *by intuition*. To know the answer to a problem without having discovered it for oneself would be like studying the map without taking the journey. Lacking the actual shock of recognition, any answer would lack the power of total conviction, the power of genuine knowing. One must arrive at the conclusion that one cannot be the doer from one's own experience.

It has to be understood very clearly that the man of total understanding must in no way be confused with the man in isolation, the glamorous man of wisdom, practicing the arts of occultism. The awakened man is clearly a very human individual: he knows the joy and misery of the moment. Anger could arise, and so also fear in the moment; he has other little 'weaknesses' of character in his programming like anyone else, he is not above falling in love or even succumbing to a temptation. The perfection of the awakened sage is to be perfectly and simply human. The significant difference is that the ordinary man is, in one way or another, at odds with his own humanness and is always attempting to be one thing or another and simply does not realise that no human being, a uniquely programmed human organism, could ever be an individual doer. That, in the words of the Buddha, "events happen, deeds are done, but there is no individual doer thereof."

The moment of awakening means the total realisation that the individual entity represented by the 'me'-entity becomes a non-entity with the sense of personal doership and responsibility totally annihilated. And yet the ego realises quite clearly that this "transparent meaninglessness can laugh and talk, eat and drink, run up and down, look at the earth and sky and all this without any sense of there being any problem, any psychological knot, in the midst of it."

Awakening almost necessarily involves a tremendous sense of relief because it brings to an end the habitual psychological cramp, created by the sense of volition or doership, of trying to grasp the mind by the mind. In time, the sense of relief must wear off, but not the awakening, unless one has confused it with something achieved; but then, that would clearly mean that the awakening has not indeed truly happened, that the sense of doership has not been truly annihilated if there is the slightest attempt to exploit the state of mind by indulging in ecstasy or deliberately using it in any way.

Awakening is thus only incidentally pleasant, or relieving or ecstatic. In itself, it is, in essence, just the ending of an artificial and absurd use of the mind. Beyond that, it is 'nothing special' since the ultimate content of awakening is never a particular object of knowledge or experience but the annihilation of the sense of doership as a separate entity.

It should be obvious that what-we-are, substantially and fundamentally, can never be a distinct object of knowledge. Awakening is to know that reality cannot be known. Awakening is to know what reality is not – *neti neti.*

In the words of a Zen Master:
    "When all the idea of self-power (as the individual doer) based upon moral values and disciplinary measures is purged, there is nothing left in you that will declare itself to be the hearer, and just because of this you do not miss anything you hear (total hearing)."

So long as one thinks about listening, it is impossible to hear clearly, and so long as one thinks about trying – or not trying – to let go of oneself, one cannot let go. Yet, it is an amusing fact that whether one thinks about listening or not, the ears do hear just the same, and nothing can stop the sound from reaching them.

Liberation from the bondage of 'time' – that is what the Ultimate Understanding means. The fact of the matter is that anything that constitutes a part of living can only happen in the present moment. Even the flash of total understanding can only happen in the moment. That moment all doubts have vanished, and one asks oneself: how could I not have seen it so far? It has always been there. It is truly quite obvious that there is no other 'time' than this instant, and that the past and the future are mere abstractions without any concrete reality.

It has always seemed that the 'present' as such really does not exist except as a minimal hairline difference between the past and the future, because our experience is that life in this world hurries by with such rapidity that it is gone before we can enjoy it. But when the 'awakening to the instant' happens, one suddenly realises with a jolt that the reverse is indeed the truth: it is rather the past and the future which are the illusions and it is the present moment, in which the experience happens, that is the eternal Real. We are surprised into the realisation that the horizontal succession of time is only a convention created by our single-track verbal thinking, a mental concept which interprets the world by grasping bits and pieces of it, labelling them happenings and events.

The fact of the matter is that every such grasp of the mind excludes the rest of the world, so that this type of comprehension can only get an approximate vision of the whole through a series of grasps. Yet the superficiality of this mind is clearly seen in the fact that it is not able to regulate even the human organism. The operation of the nerves, glands, muscles, and sense organs is so controlled not by the individual mind in the psychosomatic organism

97

but by that 'original Mind', which controls life itself in its totality.

And yet the individual mind can only be one aspect of that original Mind, and therefore, the individual mind can awaken to the eternal present moment only if it stops grasping the little pieces of life. Awareness of the present moment can come about by the same principle as the clarity of hearing and seeing and the proper freedom of the breath. Clarity of sight is just the realisation that the eyes will take in all details by themselves in the absence of the effort of the individual mind. One rests as easily in the eternal present moment as his eyes and ears respond to light and sound with the total acceptance of the concrete fact that there simply cannot be any past or future: the past is dead and the future has not happened. The simple fact is that one cannot get away from the present moment by trying to attend to it: apart from the present moment, there is no separate self that can watch it and know it. This is what Hui-Neng has to say:

"In this moment there is nothing which comes to be. In this moment there is nothing which ceases to be. Thus there is no birth-and-death to be brought to an end. Wherefore the absolute tranquillity (of *nirvana*) is this present moment."

Be still.

Let life flow.

OTHER RAMESH BALSEKAR TITLES
PUBLISHED BY YOGI IMPRESSIONS

For information on Ramesh Balsekar, visit:
www.rameshbalsekar.com


For further details, contact:
**Yogi Impressions LLP**
1711, Centre 1, World Trade Centre,
Cuffe Parade, Mumbai 400 005, India.

Fill in the Mailing List form on our website
and receive, via email, information on
books, authors, events and more.
Visit: www.yogiimpressions.com

Telephone: (022) 61541500, 61541541
E-mail: yogi@yogiimpressions.com

 Join us on Facebook:
www.facebook.com/yogiimpressions

 Join us on Instagram:
www.instagram.com/yogi_impressions

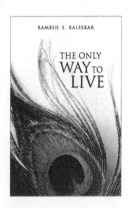
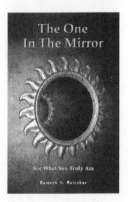